I0620574

KreAshen

The power of accepting, healing and
creating a better version of self!

LaTosha Muhammad

Copyright © Year 2025

All Rights Reserved by **LaTosha Muhammad.**

No part of this publication may be reproduced in any form, or by any means, electronic or mechanical, including photocopying, recording, or any information browsing, storage, or retrieval system, without permission in writing from LaTosha Muhammad.

ISBN
Hardcover: 978-1-965140-13-0
Paperback: 978-1-965140-14-7

Dedication

I dedicate this book to my daughters. You are the reason this book exists. God allowed me to go through a spiritual awakening, which lead to me healing and breaking a lot of generational curses. I love you more than any words, any actions can show.

I love you always and forever.
your mother

And to everyone going through childhood traumas, the dark night of the soul and spiritual awakening!! Just know you are not alone. The divine will never leave you!! Many blessings on your healing journey!!!

About the Author

Latosha Muhammad, was born and raised in Connecticut, she graduated from Sacred Heart Academy in 1997. She is a certified medical assistant and educator in phlebotomy, EKG, and medical assisting, having worked in various hospitals and doctors' offices across Connecticut. She has also taught medical certification courses at Training Direct and Nassau Community College.

Becoming a mother at 18 and having two children by 23, Latosha faced and overcame numerous challenges from her early environment. Drawing from her experiences with childhood traumas and life's hardships, she has embarked on a journey of healing. Her goal is to share her insights to assist others who have faced similar struggles.

Contents

Chapter One

The Shadows We Foster—Trauma

How I chose to go inner rather than acting out.

Generally, in the still corners of our existence, shadows often remain silent and reflective of those events that have made us who we are. These shadows, technically called trauma, are events so deeply distressing that it is formed into changing one's view and perception of things and, sometimes, even the kind of person one becomes.

Understanding trauma and its many forms can give individuals insight into their own experiences and help them feel empathy for others.

Both can be highly destabilizing and shake the ground on which we walk. Understanding the type of trauma—acute, chronic, or complex—is key to charting the path toward healing and recovery. Each type is different in characteristics, symptoms, and recovery processes.

Acute trauma comes from a single, overwhelming event that disrupts a person's sense of safety and stability. Acute trauma arises from directly experiencing or witnessing one solitary incident so awful that it is unbearably distressing. Some sources of acute trauma might be a violent attack, a car accident, or a natural disaster. Following such an event, effects are commonly immediate and may be experienced very intensely; the individual is then left dealing with the emotional aftermath.

The emotional response to the trauma of the moment may vary from shock, denial, anger, or fear—defenses practiced by the mind and body to make sense of this overwhelming experience. Physically, this might take the shape of sleeplessness, initial exhaustion, or an exaggerated startle response- responses that echo the stress response of the body. Often, these behavioral changes take the shape of retreat from social activities, inability to concentrate, or appetite changes.

Acute trauma recovery commonly consists of short-term interventions directed towards enabling the individual to deal with the stress and work through the traumatic experience. Counseling may be especially helpful, along with support groups and crisis intervention. Similarly, a good social support network from family and friends can easily make a difference in one's path to recovery.

In contrast, in chronic trauma, there is repeated and recurrent exposure over a long period. In most cases, it ranges from persistent stress to abuse situations that often leave an individual in a state of helplessness or fear for a long while. It might be caught in an abusive relationship, experiences of persistent neglect, or repeated abuse or violence.

Chronic trauma builds effects cumulatively over some period, resulting in a range of myriad emotional, physical, and behavioral symptoms. The emotional anxiety, depression, or even numbness continues in these people. Chronic trauma can cause physical conditions such as chronic pain, gastrointestinal problems, or cardiovascular health problems. Behaviorally, those facing chronic trauma can have difficulties in trust and relationships, self-integrity, and some kind of self-harm.

Recovery from chronic trauma is usually a long-term and multi-faceted approach, which is where therapy and counseling come into play, allowing the individual to process the deep-seated emotional wounds and develop coping strategies. The support groups and community resources will also provide a sense of connection and validation. Additionally, self-care toward healthy routine building is being used as one way to recover from chronic trauma.

Complex trauma, the most complicated of the three categories, refers to various, protracted, or repeated experiences that are traumatizing. They usually occur in an interpersonal setting, and they involve either abuse or neglect during sensitive developmental periods, for example, childhood. The abuse could be in the form of emotional, physical, or sexual abuse, and its perpetration is by the caretakers or significant others in someone's life.

Complex traumatic experiences cause deep, pervasive damage to emotional, cognitive, and relational functioning. An emotional level could see deep issues related to self-worth, identity, and trust. At a cognitive level, they may experience difficulties in concentration, memory, or perception of self. Complex trauma usually includes dysfunctional relationship patterns and pervasive mistrust and fear.

It is often an unfolding, day-to-day process—an amelioration involving the bottom-rung complexity between emotional and relational wounds. Trauma-informed therapy, cognitive-behavioral therapy, and EMDR are a few therapeutic methodologies that bring on healing. The base is established upon entering into a safe and supportive therapeutic relationship, within which the exploration and purging of the deeply driven effects of the trauma are to be performed.

More importantly, understanding these different types of traumas enables a framework for better understanding the unique challenges and needs that each presents. Thus, people and practitioners can navigate the road to recovery with even more strategic navigation and support the process of healing and resilience after dramatic adversity.

Understanding the type of trauma one faces can be the most important step toward healing. In working with Emily, Marcus, and Sarah, being able to identify the nature of their trauma was the first step toward healing from it. Most people recover from trauma in the process of seeking help, either from help from others, from therapy, from support groups, or self-help. Healing is associated with facing distressing feelings and memories and coming up with coping mechanisms that build resilience.

Trauma—be it acute, chronic, or complex—leaves its mark on our lives. Still, it's possible to heal and grow from even the worst experiences. Understanding the nature of our trauma and proactively striving for healing truly begins to transform our pain into strength and resilience.

As we descend into the black shadows of our own and others, let's beware that healing—is a trek. It means much patience, compassion, and dedication to understanding the intricacies of our individual experiences. In identifying and addressing our trauma, we are clearing the path for a brighter future full of hope.

While trauma casts long shadows, by courageously mustering support, self-compassion, and perseverance, it is within reach to step into the light and return to a life once lived.

The scars of trauma are such that they condition our lives in ways we often only come to understand many years later. People who face violence, coercion, and isolation at too young an age have such experiences woven into a complex and very painful tapestry of emotional and psychic suffering.

My trauma was being in a physically abusive relationship at thirteen, becoming pregnant at sixteen, and after being forced to have an abortion, becoming pregnant again at seventeen while continuing to suffer abuse and rejection from society.

When I was thirteen, I began her first 'serious' relationship, convinced that finally, I had found someone with whom I could share my love and thereby derive stability. I had been dating the guy for what I thought was an escape from home. The attention that was welcoming initially turned all dark and ugly. What started as little petty arguments went on to turn into physical abuse. The first hit was a jarring shock, and I felt a mix of disbelief and confusion at the one who said he cared for me.

How could he inflict such pain?

He even started living with us, and my mother, even after knowing that he was hurting me, allowed him to stay.

This turned the abuse into something episodic, breaking slowly but surely my sense of well-being and self-worth. Each violent act started to dissolve my definition of love and acceptance. I began to learn that I needed to deserve the abuse. That I was doing something wrong, hence the punishment. This unclear self-view scared my emotional well-being and future relationships for life.

I was barely sixteen when I learned that I was pregnant. The entire situation was very overwhelming, and my mother's strict reaction added weight to my burden. My mother was not there for me; instead, she pressured me into an abortion. I was forced into a decision that seemed to have been made for me, feeling powerless and all alone.

The abortion process was indeed very physically and emotionally traumatizing. I felt a great sense of loss—the child I had to terminate and, most importantly, the loss of control over my future and my body. Just the fact of the procedure, not to say it was carried out carelessly when, because of no consideration for my emotional state, makes my sense of betrayal and sorrow deepen beyond measure. Isolated and without family support, my emotional burden increased, adding to a traumatic experience that haunted me for years.

At seventeen, I got pregnant again. This time, though, not willing to get rid of the baby. Although I was just seventeen at that time, I bore the baby against all odds and pressures of stigma and isolation from friends and family. I felt that this step would take me closer to being in control of my life, but unfortunately, it turned out not to be so. It amplified the feelings of isolation and despair under the pressure of judgment and the inability to provide support from society.

The abuse, too, never stopped. The baby's father's behavior seemed to have transformed, and he started acting indifferently, not even caring. This abuse continued the whole pregnancy, further traumatizing and entrapping me, making me feel even more stuck. The harassment and violence did not even allow me peace and stability in life, and I, of course, could not attempt to regulate a continuous cycle of emotional and psychological agony.

This confluence of abuse—physical abuse, coerced abortion, and continued violence—left me with a more complicated trauma. The early abuse muddied my understanding of love and self-worth.

Added on top of that was the abortion, the grief, and the loss. This was another phase of the ongoing abuse presented during a second pregnancy, which carried on those feelings of helplessness and hopelessness, further deepening the cycle of trauma.

Such experiences fostered in me deep-seated problems with self-esteem, trust, and emotional stability. The constant presence of violence and isolation created feelings of worthlessness and fear that seemed to permeate everywhere. My sense of self became disfigured by the idea that I was an entity defined by the maltreatment I had faced and the fury of societal value that I was outlined by. Trauma was events; it was the emotional and psychological aftermath of such experiences as continuous strife.

Recovery from such deep trauma has to be multilevel. Therapy can also be said to be one of the vitals in healing from such. Trauma-focused therapy gives an opportunity to finally face and work through the pain, to slowly begin processing the overwhelming sense of grief, guilt, and shame, and to start rebuilding one's identity.

Trauma leaves scars, or so it seems, that can never be removed. These begin to heal upon realization. My story closely illustrates the power of facing and overcoming trauma; it is a story of where, out of the darkest moments, light and hope can be drawn.

"There is always a way out, from the deepest shadows of trauma, back to recovery and recapture of life. Supported and tenacious, it is possible to move again from the defined early trauma back into resilient, hopeful forward motion."

This, however, is a process sensitive to one's patience, courage, and readiness to revisit the hurting memory lane.

One of the first journeys on the path to recovery is when a person becomes aware of the trauma. This could be very intense, for one needs to get down to reality. Others may turn to denial or avoidance, which, logically, would seem to be a counterbalance to the effects of a disaster but usually perpetuate the suffering and delay recovery. Accepting the trauma would mean that the person recognized the fact that it drastically shaped one's life and, from this assumption, had enough respect for the self, whereby he or she acknowledges that there is a need to find healing. Not so much ruminating in the past, but rather trying to understand the influences in the present vitalizes and slowly starts the moving on process.

The most important part of any form of healing is seeking professional help. Therapy gives a structured opportunity for one to meet and process traumatic experiences. Various therapeutic approaches can be employed according to different needs. CBT enables the client to discover and work on changing the negative pattern of thoughts that relate to the trauma. EMDR helps in processing traumatic memories under a guided pattern of eye movements. Now, the focus of trauma-informed therapy is more on creating a blame-free, safe, and trustworthy environment.

Therapists address clients' emotional and mental difficulties, thereby equipping them with techniques and mechanisms to effectively deal with such a traumatic situation. They provide an atmosphere of safety in which to express oneself, gain insights about oneself, and progress along the continuum toward healing.

The journey to healing through trauma is rarely taken alone. Helping yourself build a support system is key to recovery. Support comes in many forms, but perhaps it is best sourced through support groups to access validation and a shared sense of belonging with others. The telling of one's story and the listening of another's story bring a sense of decreased isolation and often a breath of hope in how to move forward with trauma.

Support may also come from friends, family members, or mentors with whom one has a good relationship history through empathetic relational support, understandingly furnished, and in practical ways. What would greatly matter in dealing with the struggles of trauma is a network of people who really do care for one.

Self-care is doing things on purpose that maintain physical and emotional well-being. General health requires routine physical activity, a balanced diet, and sufficient sleep for higher energy and better moods. Emotional resiliency thrives when happy and relaxed through fun activities and hobbies.

Mindfulness practices like meditation and yoga help reduce stress and bring a sense of calm. In essence, self-care involves heeding one's needs and attending to them in advance to avoid the consequences of neglect. This is a process of honoring oneself and taking care of oneself during the healing journey.

Effective coping strategies can make some of the stress and emotional upheaval manageable that has become part of living with trauma. Grounding techniques, like deep breathing or progressive muscle relaxation, serve to manage anxiety and help maintain that a person stays in the present moment. Journaling thoughts and feelings provides an outlet for self-expression and access to an understanding of one's present emotional state.

These are coping strategies that lead to resilience in humans and provide a way for people to apply practical tools within their usual daily routines to manage their emotional well-being.

Healing from trauma is not linear. It is forward and about celebrating, with each small, accomplishable goal giving you a sense of having done something. For example, things you will want to be able to notice in your life on a daily basis include being able to take good care of yourself or beginning therapy. Generally, long-term goals are bigger in scope, like making more significant enhancements in relationships or growth.

Recognize the small victories and celebrate them to increase motivation and create a sense of moving forward. Understand that healing is a process, and every step, no matter how infinitesimally small, amounts to the total recovery.

Knowledge is power in the healing process. When one understands trauma and its effects, it causes an individual to make choices for recovery. When one comes to understand the nature of trauma and its impact on his or her mental/emotional status, he or she feels more in command over his or her journey to healing. Knowing efficient treatments and self-care strategies equips one with more tools to deal with the trauma and move forward.

Education reinforces the realization that post-trauma reactions are valid and that there is hope to follow. It helps one go through one's healing journey confidently and clearly.

Quite often, such trauma festers thoughts characterized by low self-esteem and dysfunctional ways of thinking. This is where it gets crucial to surface these beliefs and to challenge them. Trauma can be conceptualized as that which obviously distorts the perceptions or views about self-worth, making an individual view himself as unworthy and fearful a lot. This calls for working with a therapist in reframing such beliefs by developing a counterbalanced perception of the self as an essential component of recovery.

Finding and altering commonly held negative beliefs can help a person put himself back together again to begin working toward a healthier self-image.

Therein lies the complexity and the outsized challenge: healing from trauma is the very face of profound transformation. It's about confronting hurting memories, pushing through deep feelings, and making life-altering decisions most of the time. The road isn't at all easy, but it is one of trying to gain life back and searching for hope and fulfillment beyond the pain.

It is a personal journey: one at times horribly painful and at others full of opportunities for change, for the building up of one's essence, in the process of self-transformation, making you come out stronger. Acknowledgment, paraphrased acceptance of and reference to trauma, support system, self-care, and letting one's transformation take course are the gadgets used to shuffle an individual's movement and come out on the other side all the stronger.

Healing does not refer to forgetting the past; instead, it is about living fully even after a catastrophe. It is a journey of reclamation of the self, affinity for resilience, and finding hope amidst adversity.

Chapter Two

Toxic Shame

It begins so small that it is almost imperceptible: a shadow lurking just beyond the edge of perception. It is easily pushed away to the back of your thoughts at first: just a flashing thought, a fleeting doubt, an undefined weird feeling. Maybe that twinge of unease when you look in the mirror or that sinking feeling that follows an innocent comment from a friend.

It's the hesitation before sharing an idea in a meeting or the quick smile that hides an internal cringe after saying something wrong. These moments seem so small, so isolated and such easy things to brush off in the hustle of a given day. And yet, they are planting—and if the conditions are right, these tiny seeds begin to grow.

Its effects remain deeply rooted in so many lives. Unlike ordinary shame, which may be fleeting and tied to an event or even a behavior, toxic shame is a global sense of worthlessness and self-loathing. You don't just feel bad about something you have done; you feel bad about who you are. This kind of shame can be insidious, seeping into all areas of life, often without a person even realizing that it is there. It's that silent saboteur of self-esteem, relationships, and personal growth.

At first, it might barely be perceptible. The shadow is faint, the whispers barely audible. Seeds of doubt and discomfort go on continuously, encouraged by every mistake, every criticism, every perceived failure. It grows denser and darker. The whispers grow into a constant murmur—actually, a voice that becomes all too familiar.

'You are not good enough.'

'And you never have been, and you never will be.'

It becomes a steady presence, a background noise that's always there, no matter how hard one tries to drown it out. This isn't ordinary shame-the kind that comes and goes, tied to a specific action or event. Ordinary shame might sting, but it passes. You feel ashamed because you've done something wrong, but at least you have the ability to apologize and make amends.

You can learn from your mistakes and move forward. Ordinary shame is situational; it's temporary. But toxic shame is something altogether different. It's not about what you've done; it's about who you are. It's a deep, pervasive sense that there is something fundamentally wrong with you, something so deeply flawed that no amount of success or love or validation can ever make it right.

Toxic shame doesn't just come out of the blue. It is generally rooted in childhood and frequently within experiences that may seem inconsequential to others but are very significant to the person who lives through them. Maybe it was the critical comment of a parent, the feeling of being ignored or unimportant, or the sting of rejection by a peer. These may be very small moments when considering them alone, but together, they pile up and create the feeling that there is something wrong with you.

These experiences now begin to take root in shame. It begins to inculcate the way you begin to look at yourself and your relations with the world. You would begin to feel flawed, unlovable, and inadequate. This belief became a lens through which you view everything: your relationships, work, successes, and failures. It is always there, distorting perception and reinforcing itself every time there is a new experience.

On the other hand, the creepiest thing about toxic shame is its daily manifestations: ways it shows in the order of everyday life, quite often without you realizing it's there. It can appear as a constant neediness for approval, with a desperate desire to please everyone and absolutely everyone to prevent disfavor from you. You may then become a perfectionist, driven by a fear that any mistake will reveal the flawed self you are convinced has to be hidden at all costs. No matter how much you have accomplished, there is always that voice that says it is not enough—*that you are not enough!*

Relationships become a minefield of fear and stress. Trust is tricky, for toxic shame whispers that if people really knew you if they really could see the truth of who you are, they would leave. You fear being too open, to be vulnerable, and to be truly seen; by extension, some of your flaws obviously just might be too much for some people to bear.

However, the loneliness that comes from such self-isolation deepens the shame, making it sort of a reinforcing cycle that is impossible to really alleviate.

Toxic shame at work can be seen as both a motivator and a burden. It might motivate one toward overwork and be self-sacrificing to prove worth, but all that is ever done seems to have never been enough. You always have that nagging feeling that you are one step away from being exposed as a fraud—any day now, someone will figure out that you are not as capable as you depict yourself to be. Burnout becomes a resounding risk as you drive yourself to keep up the façade of competence and capability.

But toxic shame doesn't just affect your emotional and mental well-being. It seeps into your body, too. This stress or anxiety may come in the form of chronic tension, headache, digestive upsets, or some other problem of health. Sleep is lost because the mind continues to race with self-critical thoughts, playing over and over again each and every mistake, each and every shortcoming. The immune system is weakened and renders one susceptible to illnesses.

In extreme cases, the emotional pain of the toxic shame can actually lead someone to practice self-destructive behaviors such as substance abuse or disordered eating in an attempt to numb unbearable feelings.

And yet, toxic shame is often within plain view. It gets so internalized that it's almost as if it's part of the wallpaper of life and so, seemingly, just the way things are.

It is then so easy to mistake the symptom for character and to say to oneself, "I just can't manage relationships," "I have to try harder," or "I'll never be as sure of myself as some other person."

But these are not flaws; these are the manifestations of deep, unresolved shame.

An experience that contributed to my own toxic shame was having a boyfriend at the age of thirteen. It started out perfectly in my eyes. He would take me shopping, give me lunch money, and I would cook for him. It felt like a movie until his jealousy kicked in, and he became abusive. I would go to school with a black eye one day and a hickey the next. I was so suppressed and confused.

I remember one Valentine's Day when he brought me a cookie from Mrs. Fields at the mall. When a friend came over to hang out, he thought something was going on between us. All I remember is the cookie box hitting me across the face. He lived with me, my mom, and my little sister for a while.

I asked my mom, "Why do you let him live with us, knowing how he treats me?"

She said, "It is for our protection because we live in the ghetto."

I guess everyone needed protection but me.

Other experiences that contributed to my own toxic shame was getting pregnant at sixteen. When my mom found out, she didn't say anything to me. Instead, she made an appointment and took me to have an abortion. I had no say in what I wanted to do about my situation—I just had to go through with it. I don't think I fully processed the entire ordeal because of my age.

From that point on, I suppressed my feelings, feeling horrible about myself without really grasping what I had done. To make things worse, my mom told my boyfriend that I had moved out of town, so I couldn't see or talk to him for any type of comfort. I felt so alone and embarrassed. I believe she made me go through with it not because she cared about my well-being or health but because she wanted to maintain her perfect image.

A year later, I got pregnant again. This time, I wasn't going to let her dictate my decision, so I decided to keep my baby. I was seventeen, in my last year of high school. I attended an all-girls private school, and when the principal found out, she called me into her office. She told me that my behavior was inappropriate and that if I wanted to graduate, I would have to wear loose-fitting clothes and keep the news to myself. Again, I felt horrible, isolated, and embarrassed. This was supposed to be a happy time in my life, like in the movies, but it was anything but that.

I didn't know my daughter's father that well—we had only been dating for a few weeks when I got pregnant. He turned out to be emotionally and physically abusive. I remember him fighting with me when I was about six to eight months pregnant. He would let me walk to and from school with my heavy backpack while he drove his new car. My classmates would talk about me, asking why my boyfriend didn't give me rides. I couldn't answer them. I did have a car, but my mom would take it and disappear for days.

At the time, I didn't know it was because of her drug addiction. It was a very confusing, humiliating, and embarrassing time in my life. I worked up until the day I gave birth. I felt hopeless, shameful, lonely, worthless, and unlovable.

Though it's terrible to realize, recognizing toxic shame is the first step in healing. It is actually the power that comes from seeing inadequacy and self-loathing as feelings that are not true reflections of reality but rather as deeply ingrained beliefs that have taken hold over time.

It recognizes that the thoughts and feelings may seem so powerful and so convincing but are not the truth of who you really are. And that is when it finally dawns, one can learn to escape the hold of the toxic shame and retrieve what is inside of him, of worth and feeling whole, always there, just hidden beneath layers of self-doubt and fear.

It is a process of healing from toxic shame; it is not a point of destination. It is neither a quick fix nor an easy process. This involves taking the time and practicing self-compassion to confront the painful past and beliefs that feed into shame. In this connection, therapy may help provide a safe, supportive environment for exploring the roots of shame.

Overcoming my own toxic shame has been a journey. I started by traveling with my children, praying hard, and using positive affirmations. I began with statements like 'I am lovable,' 'I am a good person,' and 'I can do better.'

I wrote a bunch of positive affirmations on Post-it notes and stuck them to my bedroom mirror. Every time I walked by, I say them out loud. I listened to a lot of meditation music, started practicing yoga and Zumba, and found these activities really helped with my self-esteem. They forced me to look at myself in the mirror, which was very hard at first because I was so judgmental of myself. Before this, I never really looked at myself.

Reading self-help books, listening to podcasts, and writing in my journal helped tremendously too. *Dr. Gabor Maté* was a life-saver—I recommend him to anyone on a healing path. His work helped me pinpoint my traumas, understand what I developed as a result of those traumas, and begin to accept and forgive what had happened to me. Healing from toxic shame is not easy, but it's essential.

Mindfulness practices are also helpful. They quiet the relentless inner critic and, with appropriate awareness, bring the present moment into consciousness without distortions in the meanings attached to past occurrences.

A support structure is next. Toxic shame thrives in isolation, so it can feel very liberating to speak with others and share these feelings with a close friend or loved ones. It's in those moments of connection that the power of shame begins to unravel.

Hearing someone say, "I know," or "You're not alone," can be soothing to the soul. It is a reminder that the shame you're feeling is not the truth of who you are.

Self-compassion is another powerful tool in healing from toxic shame. It means treating oneself with the same kindness and understanding that one would give to a friend in pain. Everyone makes a mistake, everyone is flawed, and it does not define your worth. It allows for the possibility of forgiveness, not just from others but from oneself. It's the practice of being kind, of allowing yourself to be human, to be imperfect, to be enough just the way you are.

When you first start to heal, you may find there are actually resistive moments, moments that try to bring the old patterns of shame and self-criticism back into assertive life. These can be hard moments but will also hold key opportunities for learning. Each time you choose to speak to yourself in compassion rather than criticism, in understanding rather than judgment, you relatively weaken the mental grip of toxic shame. Over time, these new patterns become stronger and more natural until the voice of shame no longer dominates your thoughts.

The journey of healing from toxic shame is anything but linear. You will have setbacks and moments of doubt when it feels like the shame is so deeply embedded that it could never be fully let go of. But at every step, no matter how infinitesimal, you are renouncing a part of you that has lain hidden under the weight of shame. You are rediscovering your intrinsic worth, your ability to love, and your ability to be whole.

This is not a journey that needs to be walked alone. Finding that inner strength within others, through therapy, support groups, or intimate relationships, could offer the strength and uplift one needs to move forward. There is power in connection, especially in knowing that others have walked this path before and have emerged on the other side.

In time, as the process of healing unfolds, there can be profound shifts in perspective. The inner critic, once so loud and in control, begins losing its power. It is at these moments when belief or faith in one's inherent worth begins to take root that it pushes up against this toxic shame that once felt insurmountable. Those might come, and there is no doubt, but they no longer carry the same power. The old patterns of thinking and behavior start to loosen and are replaced by a new sense of self-acceptance and peace.

What healing from toxic shame asks of us isn't merely a therapeutic dose of feeling better; it's all of life. It's walking through life with confidence and authenticity, really deep down knowing you are enough. Engaging in life and others from a place of one thing: love, not fear. That is being free to pursue what is important to you and the realization of the life you wish to live without the continual burden of self-doubt.

Yes, toxic shame is a heavy burden, but it is not an inescapable fate. It is not easy, but it is possible to unlearn the messages that you will reconnect with the truth of your worth. This journey is not a walk in the park and requires much courage and commitment. A tangle of shame may be loosened, but the freedom birthed from getting that toxic shame off one's neck is worth every step. It opens a doorway into a life lived more fully—more joyfully, more connected, and with self-acceptance. And that, in itself, is a gift immeasurable.

Ultimately, healing from toxic shame is a radical act of self-love. That your history doesn't define you, your mistakes or all the lies told to you about your worth. It's the reclaiming of power, right to your being, to exist as you are—unapologetically and shamelessly. In that reclaiming, there's liberty in the natural freedom of who you are supposed to be. A freedom to live—fully and wholly unapologetically in the light of your own truth.

This is one statement that I said over and over in my head and out loud,

"To forgive yourself, you have to dissolve the shame."

Chapter Three

Limiting Beliefs

Actually, the silent saboteurs that live inside all of us—limiting beliefs—are not born but are developed through our upbringing and experiences and the society we live in. Usually, we do not even know we have them or even believe they are the truth.

They are small, intangible walls erected between us, and the true movement of our lives ceases our pursuit of becoming the whole of who we really are and abstains from all risks that shape us to become learning, growing humans. And they inform us why we are not good enough, smart enough, deserving enough, or brave enough. They feed on our worst fears, insecurities, and past failures until they become so deeply ingrained that we believe them to be facts.

Limiting beliefs are subtle, personal borders defining actions and perceptions unconsciously. They stem from a mixture of those old memories, social conditioning, and what has been internalized into a mental script stating what one believes is possible for oneself. Such beliefs are invisible borders, controlling decisions and responses in ways that one often doesn't even realize it is happening. Yet, it profoundly affects the ability to push toward goals, take risks, or even try anything new.

From the very start, limiting beliefs set up a mental environment that serves to close off options to change, so changing seems remote or impossible. Avoidance works by never contesting the belief, so the belief remains unchallenged and strengthens. These beliefs become lodged in our minds and frame who we are and what we believe while silently directing our decisions.

One of the reasons why limiting beliefs are very powerful is in the level at which they become a part of us and, more often than not, lead to practical or rational conclusions. There's a cycle of inaction, either because we fear failure or inadequacy, and it takes a change in awareness and a level of willingness to question some long-held assumptions that allow us to find the courage to act in opposition to contravening those restrictive narratives which we are accustomed to living.

I remember when I first realized that I even had limiting beliefs. It wasn't one of those deep revelations in a session of introspection or therapy but a seemingly innocuous conversation. I'd had all these beliefs, kind of carrying them around with me through the years, and they'd been influencing my life.

I had convinced myself that I wasn't good enough to do much more than what I was doing because I was so afraid of failing; I was terrified of being exposed as inadequate. Usually, that limitation comes from childhood, when we are most susceptible. Many of our lives have great roles from upbringing about how to see ourselves and how to see the world. That seed of distrust, the same, comes from what the parents, caregivers, and especially the authority figures say or do, sometimes unknowingly.

As a child, you may have been told you weren't quite as able as any of your siblings. Or maybe a teacher commented on your ability to learn certain things. The words stick. They branch out in our subconscious and, before long, become part of the story we tell ourselves. Even caring parents can unintentionally foster negative limiting beliefs. This is by inflicting upon their children the fears and anxieties of the parent's own.

A parent, dreading day-in and day out about financial stability may raise a child who grows up believing that money is always scant or even impossible to acquire. In my situation, my negative limiting beliefs can be traced way back to my childhood. I always grew up in a house where criticism was more common than praise and where mistakes were met with harsh words rather than understanding. My parents were not cruel, but they went around thinking that pointing out flaws would bring me up to do better.

But the opposite effect was what it brought about instead. I thought of myself as never good enough; no matter how hard I tried, I would always fall. This kind of thinking followed me all the way into adulthood and expressed itself in everything: career choices, personal relationships, and workplace relationships. I doubted my ability to achieve and thus stayed away from any opportunity that had the potential of putting me out of my comfort zone.

As for the workplace, I would accept less in life as long as people and society accepted that is a great start for me, deep down I didn't feel worth loving and respecting because, as society also does, sometimes make its contribution to the formation of limiting beliefs in our minds. We hear voices telling us who to be and how to live from an early age.

We are indoctrinated by the media, by our friends, and by the culture we're obliged to walk in. We're told about success, about behavior, and what's right. With women, there are layered expectations around beauty, behavior, and striving for things. Two important lessons were thereby taught to us, explicitly and implicitly: that our worth lies in our appearance, our relationships, and our ability to please others; males must be strong, unemotional, and successful at whatever cost.

These societal expectations end up reinforcing the limiting beliefs we hold, making us feel that if we don't fit into these boxes, somehow, we are flawed or inadequate. I remember the social forces that fed into my own limiting thoughts. I felt like a failure. My self-worth had become so wrapped up in my head that I thought I wasn't worthy of love or happiness if I weren't what others expected me to be.

This always led to some really unhealthy behaviors and a vicious cycle of self-sabotage. Limiting beliefs don't just pop into your mind from nowhere; they are often a result of some traumatic experience or failed experience. When we fail at attempting to do something and, if that failure is public or embarrassing, then we tend to reinforce that belief: that is, we live out in life believing that we indeed cannot do it or are not good enough. We eventually even stop trying and are sure in our hearts that it will always be this way.

I internalized my failure by saying to myself that I'm really not cut out for anything; in other words, I don't have what it takes to be successful. For all the years that were to follow, I ran away from taking anything new for fear of failing.

One of the insidious ways in which limiting beliefs affect you is through creating self-fulfilling prophecies. When you believe you are not capable, you act in a way that serves to confirm that lack of ability, possibly by never putting yourself forward for the thing that is required to activate something new, never taking the risk, and never aiming for the stars. And when it doesn't work out, you point to evidence that you were right after all, and the cycle can be really tough to break; however, it is not impossible.

My childhood trauma launched the seeds of some deep feelings of toxic shame and limiting beliefs that haunted me well into adulthood. They left me feeling terrified, angry, and resentful towards life, the people around me, and the unfairness of it all. I was confused and hurt, and that guided me along the path of addiction as a way of dealing with all these overwhelming emotions that I could not express or find a clue to at that time.

Alcohol became a quick fix; I abused it regularly to numb the pain for as long as it would take. Smoking weed soon became the way to escape some reality that felt just too heavy to bear. Food, too, would become a friend and an enemy. I developed eating disorders, at one end bingeing myself into vomiting and then fasting for days as a form of self-punishment. I would swing wildly between two extremes, an easily visible proof of my inner turmoil. The physical addictions were brutal enough, but perhaps even more stifling were the mental addictions.

I became co-dependent, clinging to others in hopes that they would fill the gaping void inside me. Depression was my best friend-it dragged me down with an iron hand. My self-esteem was all but nonexistent. I basically sabotaged myself in every aspect of my life because I thought I never deserved success, love, or happiness.

People-pleasing became the only way to survive because if I did not waste an ounce of energy trying to please people at any cost, they would surely see just how worthless I actually was. I lived all my life fearing rejection and abandonment.

The first step to free up from limiting beliefs is to be aware of their presence. It is not very easy since, as I mentioned earlier, they sound like the truth. Once you start to listen to your self-story, you begin noticing patterns. Mine started when I started to ask myself questions whenever doubts crept into my mind.

Why do I believe that I am not good enough?

Where did this belief come from?

Is that actually true, or is it something I have been telling myself for so long that it feels true?

Actually, another thing that helped me break the cycle of unfounded beliefs was to practice countering the belief itself. So, if I thought I wasn't good enough, I'd remind myself of several ways in which, in fact, I was good enough.

If I believed that in some way, I wasn't worthy of love, I would think about the people in my life who loved and cared for me. This started changing by zeroing in on the evidence that contradicted the limiting beliefs.

Sometimes, you have to change how you think. Instead of seeing a mistake or a failure as proof that you're not capable, see this as an opportunity for growth. This was a game-changer for me.

But with time, I learned that the experience had been a lesson, lessons I would carry on into other ventures. Failure did not define me; instead, it gave me a step up to try once more, this time a little wiser and resilient. Breaking free from shattering beliefs does not come overnight. It takes time, effort, and loads of self-compassion. Sometimes, there are days when my old belief creeps back in and whispers into my ear that I am not good enough and I am incapable of doing things.

But now, the difference is that I know them as what they really are—beliefs and not facts. And every day that goes by gives me even greater power with which to challenge them, to transcend the fear and doubt that had held me prisoner for so very long. But probably of all the things I have learned on my journey is that we are not controlled; we are not shaped by the past or beliefs sustained all these years.

We can rewrite our stories, even the limitations of beliefs that no longer serve us, and create new ones to empower ourselves to live the life we really want. It's not easy, but it's worth it. It is there, on the other side of those limiting beliefs, that freedom lies: the freedom to pursue your dreams, to value your worth, and to live a life not defined by fears but by possibility.

Looking back, I think if it hadn't been for my children, it might have pushed me to a point where I would have lost all hope. They were my lifeline in times when I was drowning. It was the one thing I clung to in such dark moments. Maybe getting them early on in life would have saved me from losing myself completely.

With them, too, I walked life behind a cloak of isolation, forever inexcusable and always hiding the truth of what I was going through. I remember walking around with my toes bent up—a subconscious habit that reflected just how much tension and anxiety I carried inside. My eyes were often red and bulgy from crying, so I would lie to people, saying that it was allergies or that I was just exhausted working and taking care of my children. I built elaborate lies, anything to keep the truth buried, because I was absolutely terrified of what people would think if they knew the reality inside of me. I felt so completely alone, even when surrounded by others.

Today, I still battle with many of these demons, in particular, alcohol and food. It seems almost instinctive: whatever will make me feel better about myself if I'm happy will celebrate, whether it's drinking or having a meal. If I am sad, a drink or a meal numbs me. Many of these things I've discovered come from being bored, focusing too much on the past, or how people have wronged me.

Therefore, gradually, I could detect these triggers and heighten my understanding of myself and my tendencies over the years. I push it away or distract myself when I feel that I want to overeat or overdrink. Actually, I find that if I distract myself for just twenty to thirty minutes, my brain can reroute, and the cravings pass. Instead of eating or drinking, I started walking in the mornings, doing activities with my children, reading more, and visiting places that I wanted to but never had!! These healthy alternatives helped tremendously with my addictions.

It's not always easy, but awareness is the first step toward healing, and every day, I'm working on being kinder to myself!

Chapter Four

Addiction

Addictions are multilayered and complex; they cross into all areas of human experience. At the core of addiction lies an overwhelming compulsion that often supersedes one's rational thinking and emotional life. It can be substance-oriented, activity-oriented, or behavior-oriented. Through the addictive cycle, the person gets caught in a self-destructive pattern that is hard to break out of.

The journey into addiction is often tumultuous and deeply intertwined with personal history, particularly trauma. Understanding the nature of addictions has to do with understanding how trauma underlies their beginning and how treatment of trauma becomes a way to overcome addiction.

Addiction comes in all forms. People generally relate addiction to substance abuse, such as alcohol, drugs, or prescription medications, but that's just about it. Other examples of addictions are gambling, shopping, food, and sex. The behavioral addictions, though less talked about, are as disabling. They have the same power to hijack one's life and wreak havoc on relationships, careers, and self-esteem. The operating principle behind any addiction is that it makes the individual compulsively continue with the behavior regardless of the negative consequences involved.

It is essential to differentiate between habit and addiction. A habit is a behavior repeatedly carried out, while addiction can be described as that behavior being compulsively repeated to satiate a psychological or emotional need. An addiction makes one resort to relief through a certain behavior or substance from stress, anxiety, or deep emotional pain. It is often a coping mechanism for an unaddressed trauma that has found its way into the person's psyche.

At such moments of addiction, the chemistry of the brain is changed, and one stops making rational decisions; instead, one is compelled by an emotional state, often notwithstanding adverse consequences. It differs from habit mainly in that addiction usually contains an element of loss of the person feels unable to stop or cut down on the behavior even when he realizes the damages of it. Such lack of control is one of the hallmarks of addiction; this is almost always accompanied by intense wanting and withdrawal symptoms when the addictive activity or substance has been removed.

Addictions do not happen overnight; more often than not, they are subtle and work their way into a person's life until they are so deeply ingrained. The beginning appeal of the addictive substance or behavior tends to bring relief or, instead, escape from stress, pain, and trauma. As time goes by, however, this relief becomes more challenging to achieve, and it is only achieved by taking in more of the addictive substance or repetition of the addictive behavior. This is called tolerance, and the deeper the tolerance is, the more profound the addiction.

The connection between trauma and addiction has been documented. Things that occurred during growing up, such as neglect or abuse, or later on, like the loss of a loved one, violence, or chronic stress, leave an indelible emotional and psychological mark. When trauma is unresolved or untreated, it is pretty common for individuals to turn to means of numbing the pain or trying to escape from those feelings that are associated with their traumatic experience. Addictive behaviors or substances provide momentary relief but, in the long term, contribute to an increase in pain.

Many of those suffering from addiction had complex trauma. Complex trauma is considered the trauma in which the person experiences multiple, usually prolonged, traumatic experiences that normally start at an early age. Some may have grown up in unstable homes where they are physically, emotionally, or sexually abused, or they may witness domestic violence or be chronically neglected.

These experiences may cause emotional wounds and leave them with the feeling of not being good enough, full of shame, and powerless from the bottom of their hearts. Without any healthy coping mechanisms, support, or healthy expressions, such feelings may lead them to substance use or behavior that comforts them for a short time from their inner turmoil.

This is not to suggest that anyone who experiences trauma will eventually develop an addiction. Still, the linkage is close enough that trauma-informed approaches to addiction treatment are becoming more widely recognized. These methods realize that for many people, addiction is a way to cope-to offset the overwhelming pain and distress caused by past trauma-and therefore, treating their addiction does involve addressing the underlying trauma that drives the addiction.

Recovery from addiction is not a linear process but is somewhat different for each individual. There are, however, some steps that are universally considered to be the very basics in overcoming addiction. Probably foremost among these would be simply acknowledging that there is a problem. The force of denial can be vital in addiction.

Most people fail to realize the severity of their addiction, or they do not consider and admit to themselves and others that they have lost control. Denial indeed calls for a very profound level of self-reflection and honesty, which in many cases is compelled by a 'rock bottom' where the effects of the addiction get so unbearable.

The second thing would be seeking help once the problem has been recognized. This can be through professional counseling or rehabilitation programs or even through support groups like Alcoholics Anonymous and Narcotics Anonymous.

What they all share in common, however, is the notion that recovery seldom, if ever, occurs in a vacuum. Addiction tends to live in secrecy and isolation, so breaking free from it often requires the support, accountability, and encouragement of others. Seeking help is not a sign of weakness; it is a sign of strength sign of taking responsibility for one's healing.

For many, recovery is sometimes wrapped up with a combination of therapy and medication. Individual therapy can help an individual explore the roots of addiction that underlie their addiction, primarily when the causes are related to trauma. Cognitive-behavioral therapy, for instance, is usually used in an attempt to help the person identify and alter those thinking patterns and actions that contribute to their becoming addicted.

On the other hand, addiction due to trauma can also be treated more accordingly with other methods of therapy, such as dialectical behavior therapy or eye movement desensitization and reprocessing.

In some cases, medications can be utilized to either stabilize an individual during withdrawal or reduce cravings. Examples of this include methadone or buprenorphine for opioid addiction and medications like naltrexone that reduce the urge to drink alcohol. None of these pharmaceuticals treat the addictive illness; they are the bridge a person in recovery can use to stabilize their lives and then work on their long-term healing.

Another very relevant aspect of recovery is the development of new, healthy coping mechanisms. Addiction often replaces healthier ways of dealing with stress, pain, or emotional hurt; therefore, part of recovery is to learn new ways of coping with life.

This may include mindfulness practices, meditation, exercise, or creative activities such as art and writing. Equally important will be the development of a solid network of supportive friends, family members, or a community of fellow recovering people. There simply is no substitute for those who can understand the struggles of addiction and may offer encouragement as one struggles to stay on the right track.

Perhaps one of the more overlooked parts of recovery has to do with self-forgiveness and compassion. Addiction can lead to overwhelming feelings of guilt and shame, not only about the addictive behaviors but also regarding having allowed the addiction to take hold in the first place. This is where self-compassion comes in-the realization that addiction does not define any particular person. It is one response of many to pain and trauma, not some personal moral failing. Learning to forgive oneself for the past is a crucial step toward going forward to live a healthier, addiction-free life.

For many people, spirituality is an essential part of recovery. This does not necessarily mean religion, though for some, religious faith may be a source of strength. In that sense, spirituality is the broader scope regarding the feeling of relatedness to something more significant than the self, which might be nature, the universe, or some supernatural power.

This can encourage persons in recovery to feel supported by something and give them more meaning in living their lives. Such practices include prayer, meditation, or spending time in nature. They can be very helpful as a source of peace and strength.

The recovery process also requires a commitment to ongoing self-awareness. Addiction is a disease; recovery implies being recovered for the rest of one's life, entailing continued vigilance against recurrence. This does not mean living in constant fear of relapse but rather maintaining an awareness of triggers and vulnerabilities. Relapse for many is often part of the recovery journey, and though it may feel like a setback, it does not mean failure. What is important is a person's response to a relapse: through recommitment to recovery and learning from the experience.

Recovery from addiction is a journey into self-discovery and transformation. It is much more than just abstaining from the addictive substance or behavior; it's about healing that more profound pain that perhaps caused the addiction in the first place. To many people, recovery is a different way of life, more connected, present, and authentic. This is a journey that requires so much courage, strength, and resilience to face off not just the addiction but also the more profound emotional wounds that perhaps fueled it in the first place.

Lastly, overcoming addiction means the reclamation of one's life. This speaks of breaking loose from the chains that have held him back from living a life with more freedom and possibility. Recovery is never easy; the pathway to it is mainly begrimed with setbacks and challenges.

It is a pathway of hope and transformation, nonetheless. One can break the vicious circle of addiction if supported rightly with the right tools and commitment to healing. It might take some time, but every step leads a person closer to wholeness and peace in life.

When you gain self-awareness, you change your thoughts and interpretation, and by that, you change your emotions.

Chapter Five

Codependency

Co-dependency is defined as psychological dependence on others for emotional validation and, therefore, self-worth. Co-dependence usually tends to be intertwined with deep insecurities and dysfunctional dynamics of the relationship. People who are afflicted with co-dependency are not able to develop healthy, reciprocal relationships because they tend to concentrate their energies on satisfying someone else's needs at the cost of their well-being.

These behaviors typically stem from unresolved emotions connected to childhood, such as parental or household dysfunction and emotional neglect. Such early manifestations automatically lead to unhealthy attachment styles wherein a person seeks validation and approval outside of themselves.

The symptoms can be extremely different with many co-dependents but often include feelings of low self-esteem, an overwhelming fear of abandonment, and a desperate need to control. Some of these individuals will feel guilty as if it is they who are in charge of others' happiness or unable to set appropriate boundaries, as the very definition of themselves is somewhat entwined with the well-being of others. Co-dependents often find themselves playing the rescuer in their relationships, compulsively trying to fix the problems of others. This role can easily cause chronic stress and burnout, as their needs are constantly sacrificed to care for others.

A second characteristic of co-dependency is an almost desperate need to please others at almost any cost. Co-dependent persons fear conflicts and criticism at any price, thinking that this very conflict can provoke rejection or abandonment. This makes them suppress their needs and opinions and their very wills, which can escalate into hatred and resentment in the long run. They become too responsible by assuming that they have to regulate situations or people so as not to create chaos or misery. This desire for control can look like micromanaging, enabling, or manipulating other people, even subconsciously.

Relationships-Dependence or co-dependent behavior, presented as an unhealthy equilibrium, when the two parties develop an over-reliance on each other for emotional support, approval, or validation. It creates dependency upon another and makes the co-dependent person insist on constant affirmations received from his or her partner, friend, or relative. In contrast, the other person may be exploited or burdened by one's constant attention. Such a dependent person is, therefore, usually made to feel worthless or empty unless they are actively involved in meeting someone else's needs. This will make them put the relationship above all things.

The signs of co-dependency in relationships usually start subtly but become stark as the dynamic advances. The most evident and prevailing indication is that such a person cannot function without someone else. Since the co-dependent may be in decision-making as a direct consequence of seeking validation and approval from his or her partner, a decision may be hard for him or her to make. They also lack good emotional acknowledgment and expression of their feelings because they feel more for the other person's emotional state than their own. Poor emotional autonomy results in weak lines, thus unspoken personal boundaries, making them responsible for a partner's thoughts, emotions, and actions.

Another big behavioral characteristic of a co-dependent is that she sacrifices her own needs and wants for the other. She does not fulfill or chase her hobbies, interests, or dreams and aims for the achievement of those but always co-chases the aspirations of her partner. Such self-sacrifice often goes unrewarded or is even punished and culminates in feelings of frustration or sadness. These have repercussions that can cause the dependent person to feel they are trapped in the relationship because their identity is becoming increasingly tied to the role of a caregiver or supporter.

People with co-dependence tend to fear losing some aspect of their life and have a huge fear of solitude or abandonment, and might stay in bad or abusive relationships. They are more than likely to tolerate abuse or abandonment by their partner because they believe they are solely responsible for saving the relationship no matter what. Abandonment fear also makes them clingy or possessive because they have fears that their partner will leave them sometime in the future. They go to great lengths at trying not to let things get worse and can even sacrifice themselves for a conflict-free existence and avoid separation from their partners.

Co-dependent relations create emotional enmeshment that can become very draining to both ends. In the instance of being unable to cope with the emotional needs of his/her partner, a co-dependent becomes increasingly anxious or depressed. In contrast, his/her partner is perceived to be still being suffocated and overwhelmed by constant demands for attention and support. This can lead to a communication breakdown because the co-dependent person cannot clearly address his/her needs or feelings to his/her partner, whereas the latter feels helpless in getting the emotional space in the relationship.

To gain self-awareness, you have to practice focusing on personality and behavior.

Mostly, co-dependency creates a cycle of enabling because a co-dependent unwittingly allows and fosters an unhealthy behavior in his/her partner. For example, they over-accept the role of carrying another person's errands by lying on his or her behalf or even shielding him or her from the effects of his or her decision. This brings about a vicious circle because the partner may become so dependent on the co-dependent for advice or practical care, and the co-dependent is hardwired into the caregiver role.

Many of the most challenging aspects of co-dependency are that those in these patterns of behavior cannot seem to break themselves free. Co-dependent individuals often can't see how dependent they are themselves because they have been taught to center more around others' needs and desires. They may feel guilty or ashamed for focusing on themselves, as they are certain that doing so would be selfish or unloving. This leads to quite an easy lack of ability to set boundaries or for healthier relationship dynamics.

Codependency, therefore, by definition, becomes a dysfunctional relationship dynamic wherein one person is the giver, giving up their needs, desires, and well-being to fill the demands of the other party, a taker. The giver becomes lost in people-pleasing throughout their life cycle with a mode of saying 'yes' to every request and putting the needs of the taker above their own. The taker is comfortable in this situation and keeps on taking without giving back. Such a relationship is almost one-way as the giver gets drained and emotionally exhausted, while the taker remains unmoved, even oblivious or uninspired by the harm being enacted.

Codependency can take several forms. While it is commonly associated with an intimate relationship, it is not limited to a love scenario. This can occur between parents and children, between family members of the same household, through friendships, or even in the workplace, where an employee may consistently work themselves to an extreme trying to fulfill the needs of a supervisor or coworkers. The essential underlying point, regardless of the context, is one person sacrifices at their own expense, and the other person takes less apparent effort to give.

In these relationships, the giver tends to overinvest themselves not only in their provider role but also in the relationship as a whole. Such people control both ends of the relationship and often ensure that the taker's needs are satisfied while possibly neglecting their own emotional, physical, or financial well-being. This really creates a deep level of frustration and resentment for the giver because he then realizes that the more he gives, the closer they get but still more he has to give, the imbalanced relationship will still remain, and the needy taker will keep asking for more.

Personal experiences usually reveal a great deal regarding the pain caused by codependency. I view this happening in my relationships with my five uncles, who all happen to be alcoholics or drug abusers, using me to give and help them in every possible manner. They used my house rent-free and took food from my table, even taking things from my home that belonged to me and my children.

Even with all this, I allowed them to keep coming back, thinking it was my duty to take care of them. Nothing was in my favor-no thankfulness, no reciprocity, not even a tone of respect for the concessions that were being made. Rather, it became a vicious cycle of give and take where it was I who always emerged on the short end.

Co-dependent relationships make you feel like you are resentful, worthless, and unappreciated. It eats away at your self-esteem until you feel like you have no value unless you are giving. Abuse is tolerated more often in this kind of relationship at a level that would be unthinkable outside the codependent dynamic. You will tell yourself this is what you deserve or it's just your responsibility to keep sacrificing. This way of thinking makes it all too easy to forget your worth and the whole concept of setting boundaries.

To a person, codependency starts with experiences one has while growing up in dysfunctional homes. The relationship dynamics experienced early on in life often set the patterns for how we will engage later in life.

My own case of codependency ran very deep, and my roots came from my own background of dysfunction. It bound us all together - chaos and trauma. And the dysfunctional environment taught me that giving endlessly was the way to maintain relationships. It wasn't until much later in life that I realized the patterns in my behavior and how very, very deeply tied they are to early experiences.

Typically, codependency is positively reinforced through limiting beliefs, childhood traumas, and deep toxic shame. It conditions you to believe that whatever value you might have lies in the amount you can give or how well you can manage the emotions and needs of others. This dynamic is especially nasty because it takes away your ability to think about yourself as being worthy of love and care unless you are constantly sacrificing for someone else.

With these scenarios, I entered my marriage. My husband was constantly going to and from jail and out of jail, and I'd rush to get him out of jail. I'd drive up and down the highway to visit him, send money, write letters and provide for whatever he needed. For all this, I received nothing: no love, no empathy, no appreciation of what I did. I was putting out all my energy at my own expense and ended up worthless. It wasn't until I started to really think about what's happened that I realized how quickly and intricately a pattern of codependency can take hold in a relationship.

Part of the insidious nature of codependency is how it makes you manage both your own emotions and the emotions of others. You focus so much on pleasing the other, making sure they're comfortable to begin with, that you forget your own feelings. This means you do not want to feel that this taker is going to go through what you feel-it's emptiness-so you try to make everything easy for them, facilitate their dependency.

But by so doing, you are really keeping both yourself and the taker from growing. The giver is stuck in this cycle of self-denial, whereas the taker will never have the pressure of dealing with their issues because the world is just constantly pushing the envelope to make that possible for them.

Codependency is a vicious circle of giving and taking. There's, however, a way out of it to heal and take off. First of all, you have to recognize the imbalance, then define the limits you need to draw between you and the other person that should protect you. It's painful, but this process enables you to rebuild your self-esteem and grow into the next phase of life.

It takes extraordinary self-awareness and, often, emotional healing just to get out of co-dependency. It involves recognizing, interpreting, and finding ways to overcome the root causes that often accompany the dependency pattern of self-esteem, abandonment fears, or even unresolved trauma. Therapy or counseling may be involved, and that is the point where they can open up topics related to the root causes of their co-dependent behavior. Healing, learning to say no, knowing how to make one's needs known, and being able to set boundaries enables a person to reassert him/herself and create more balanced and mutually fulfilling relationships.

Therapy, apart from self-care, is a method through which an individual can overcome co-dependency. It might include learning how to take care of one's emotional and physical needs, engage oneself in hobbies or passions, and develop self-esteem that has nothing to do with others. Developing a strong sense of identity and self-compassion will develop a feel for one's intrinsic value and worth irrespective of his role in a relationship and, therefore, help break the cycle of co-dependency.

This pattern is deeply ingrained, yet it is not insurmountable. Self-awareness can lead to healing at the emotional level and, hence, a commitment to personal growth, capable of leading individuals to learn how to establish healthier, more fulfilling relationships founded on mutual respect, autonomy, and emotional interdependence. Patience and self-compassion are necessary because, often, the help sought will involve unlearning long-held beliefs and behaviors. Still, it will result in a much greater sense of emotional freedom and well-being.

Co-dependency can manifest in the most ordinary friendship, within a family, or even at work. Common to all these connections and relationships, however, is a lack of emotional autonomy and a tendency to derive self-value from the acceptance or validation by other people. The only shift that could make someone free from co-dependency is looking the other way about self-worth to value themselves for who they are, not what they can be to others.

That's not such an easy shift since, generally, people need to deal with how other people believe in regard to worth and love, but it is very important for the construction of more sound and balanced relationships.

For a very long time, I enabled my uncles by giving them whatever they wanted, although it came at my own and my children's expense. By continuously bailing them out, I was letting them get through all of life without having to fulfill one ounce of responsibility.

I never had to be responsible for myself because they could always bail out each other. It was only when I set the boundaries and cut off the enabler behavior in the lives of my uncles that I found the start of healing from the destruction codependency caused within me.

Boundaries are very important elements in recovery from codependency. In my case, it would involve stopping all contact with the uncles. I came to realize that no one would go on to steal from me repeatedly without being checked upon for some form of punishment. It was painful, but at the same time, it was one of those decisions necessary for self-healing.

The hardest thing was the perception that I would never be able to receive so much as a sorry or acknowledgment from them for all they perpetrated against me. In codependent relationships, a taker rarely acknowledges what they may be doing wrong, so soliciting their validation is going only to drag out the anguish.

I had to set a boundary with other members of my family, including my mother. Yes, I still have a relationship with her, but she cannot belittle me or talk down to me. Whenever she starts criticizing or attacking me verbally, I instantly hang up the phone or stop the conversation. Setting such limits was an important step toward regaining my self-esteem and healing from the damage that codependency had caused.

Healing from codependency is, however, a long process and calls for many self-reflections and emotional works. For me, I had to rely on the advice of a few YouTubers, such as Dr. Ani and Lisa Romano, whose contents explained a lot about codependency dynamics and how to be free from them. I stopped providing solutions unless they requested them. I let them make their mistakes.

Thus, I started regaining my life and getting the first chance in years to satisfy

all my needs.

Chapter Six

Self-sabotage

Self-sabotage is characterized as behavior and thoughts that are harmful to one's interest and/or development. It is the act of unintentionally or unconsciously undermining your own goals, happiness, or success. It's our behavior, our thoughts of involuntary or unconscious nature, that are harmful to our interests and development. It's very harmful to our unconscious mind.

Fundamentally, Self-sabotage arises from fears, insecurities, and unresolved issues. These issues push a person to practice negative self-talk. Some people might avoid things like promotions or new jobs, thinking that they do not deserve any success. This creates a loop where the person keeps sinking into this negative self-talk.

Thoughts and feelings are tied to behavior.

Self-sabotage may extend beyond immediate setbacks. It sometimes creates a pattern in the person's relationships and careers that causes them to fall. The unconscious mind has a huge role in the formation of this pattern. People stay in this cycle of self-sabotage and frustration without even realizing it.

Noticing and recognizing self-sabotage is primary for healing. This often involves therapy and other mental health practices. By understanding the hidden meaning behind negative self-talk, people can progress toward healing.

Some other ways we manifest self-sabotage in our lives are by procrastinating, forgetting deadlines, failing to prepare for tests or events, refusing to ask for help when we need it, setting unrealistic goals, and starting things like classes, projects, and jobs but never completing them. Not finishing deadlines is also a form of self-sabotage. It stems from anxiety and stress. When a person overlooks an important date, they feel overwhelmed and frustrated, and this makes it harder for them to follow up on responsibilities. People with self-sabotaging mindsets fail to prepare for tests or important events. This lack of preparation results in poor performance, which further reinforces the negative self-talk about their capabilities.

Many people struggle when asking for help. Sometimes, it's the complete refusal, and others, it's the denial of being in trouble. This leads to isolation and stressful situations. It also affects the person's relationships. They also set unrealistic goals and aim too high. This would invoke feelings of discouragement and frustration when these goals are not met.

This cycle of stagnant progress reinforces negative self-talk and creates a negative self-identity where the person is constantly under the feeling of worthlessness. Acknowledging these patterns is very important to start the process of healing. By addressing them, a person starts to accept that they have something to work on and it drives them forward to seek help.

Another name for self-sabotage is behavioral dysregulation. Self-sabotaging is usually a way to cope with fears and failures. With everything I went to, self-sabotaging was something that I fell prey to. I would often make a list of goals that I knew, in my mind, were unrealistic. I would start a class knowing well that I wouldn't be able to complete it and then would stop taking it in the middle. This would give me a reason to criticize myself for the fact that I did not complete my goals. I repeatedly would tell myself that I didn't have it in me to do any of this, and that's why I kept failing. Self-sabotaging works against you almost all of the time.

Some psychological causes of self-sabotage are past traumas, low self-esteem, lack of control, negative self-talk, and undeveloped coping skills. Overthinking has been my number one self-sabotage. I would overthink about my wrongdoings, about my past, and about the wrongdoings of others toward me. This tendency to overthink extended to areas of my life where I felt uncertain, particularly around finances and situations beyond my control. Instead of taking action, I would overthink and become anxious, which would throw me into the self-doubt cycle. With each thought, I spiraled into negative self-talk. I would tell myself that I wasn't capable of handling my life. This behavior caused a heavy emotional burden and made it difficult to process what was going on in the present.

Becoming aware of it helped me confront these thoughts and work towards healing.

Overthinking is a deep fear of loss of control.

Our thoughts are tied to our behavior. If we change our thought processes, we can definitely change our behavior.

Self-sabotage affects relationships, especially intimate relationships. Relationships that lack vulnerability and trust easily break when one of the partners has self-sabotaging tendencies. My marriage was affected by Self-sabotage as well. Both me and my husband showed signs of being self-saboteurs, which led to many misunderstandings and conflicts. I noticed that I was very avoidant in the beginning, especially when it came to issues between us. I shied away from difficult conversations and confrontations Instead of holding myself accountable for my actions, I would trap myself in a negative mindset where I would only focus on the negative sides of our relationship. I fixated on what my husband should've done and not on how I should've reacted.

I would pick fights with him over small issues. I would bring up the past and reopen old wounds. This gave rise to more conflicts and also created a resentful environment. The fact that I kept thinking about the past meant that I couldn't appreciate the present. Each argument took me back two steps. These fights ultimately took us to the point where we had little to no communication between us. We fought all the time and became defensive. I often felt misunderstood, which led to more negative self-talk.

People ask why someone would self-sabotage. The answer is that if someone does self-sabotage because they have been hurt in their past, they have been let down. People with self-sabotaging tendencies have low self-esteem and undeveloped coping skills, all from past trauma.

Healing from self-sabotage is a hard thing. One of the ways I healed from it was that I noticed my negative thought patterns. It helped me understand and figure out my way of thinking when I encountered a tough situation.

The way to do it is that whenever you get reminded about your past, whether it be through a random song or a random thing in your daily routine, anything that hurts you or has traumatized you, you quickly counter it with another thought. Noticing my negative thoughts has helped me to change them right away and start thinking about where I am and where I want to be in the future. This has taken years to develop. I started to have patience with myself. Whenever I would have negative thoughts, and I would lash out, I said to myself. 'It's okay. At least I acknowledge where I went wrong.' I started to observe my behavioral pattern and how certain environments and people would have me think about the past or anything related to it. I noticed that whenever I got bored, I would start thinking of my past trauma. I started paying attention to the smallest of things, like certain alcoholic beverages. I noticed if I drink certain alcohol, I would have a certain behavioral experience. This observation really helped me understand my healing process.

Another way of healing from this was exercising and getting out in nature. I would get outside a lot. I would walk on the ground with my bare feet in the grass. I would often take part in sun gazing. Things like these helped me a lot to heal.

Healing from Self-sabotage is a slow journey and a personal one. It changes your life significantly. Cognitive-behavioral therapy is often used to identify these kinds of behaviors, and a therapist helps you counter them using CBT. But CBT is not the only option. Some therapists stress the use of Dialectical-behavior therapy, which focuses on emotional regulation. It helps you manage intense feelings and improves your relationship. This helps a lot with people who have self-sabotaging tendencies that are tied to emotional dysregulation or communicational issues.

Group therapy is also a way to conquer negative self-talk. Being around people who went through or are going through the same issues as you are helps you normalize your feelings. It provides insight into your own thought process. It creates an environment where you are allowed to be vulnerable collectively.

Physical activities also help with healing. Yoga and dance therapy are becoming mainstream practices that help you reconnect with your body. It releases stored tension and emotions that sometimes lead to negative self-talk, which further leads to self-sabotaging behaviors. These activities help you ground yourself and start or further the healing process.

Having a routine that prioritizes self-care can help in healing too. Forming healthy habits like exercising regularly, sleeping well, and having balanced nutrition can improve and maintain that healing process. Feeling well physically significantly improves your mental health, which helps you fight or counter negative self-talk.

Perusing creative hobbies like art and music helps in healing, too. Music, art, writing, or any form of self-expression allows you to process emotions in a healthy way. It serves as an outlet for your feelings and creates a sense of accomplishment.

Mindfulness can also be valuable for managing stress and anxiety, particularly associated with self-sabotage. Mindfulness-based stress reduction (MBSR) combines mindfulness meditation and physical activities like yoga, which helps you create a sense of awareness of your thoughts and feelings. This approach helps you deal with your issue using a clear mindset.

Working with a mentor or coach who understands your issue can help you understand your feelings better. They provide guidance and support which directly helps you. They help you set goals that are achievable which creates a sense of accomplishment. This encourages you to set more realistic goals in the future.

Gratitude is the ultimate way to get rid of negative thoughts. It shifts your focus to a more positive outlook. By reflecting on the things you are grateful for, you focus on what's important, which helps you grow and acts as a counter to self-sabotage.

The healing process is not easy, and setbacks are very common. When you are dealing with issues that have been pulling you down for years, it is very easy to fall into their trap once you have started the healing journey. You have to embrace your journey and be compassionate to yourself. With persistent efforts, you will lessen the chances of having setbacks.

Emotional intelligence is another factor that is significant in the healing process. When you are aware of your emotions and where they stem from, you are considered emotionally intelligent. Emotional intelligence increases with self-observation. With increased emotional intelligence, you have increased chances of catching yourself falling into self-sabotage. It also goes hand in hand with practicing empathy toward yourself.

Therapists help you explore your attachment styles when you have issues regarding your relationships and self-worth. There are four styles of attachment: secure, anxious, avoidant, and disorganized. Identifying which attachment style you have can help you understand what issues run deep in your relationships. It is a great way to catch self-sabotaging behaviors in any type of relationship.

In addition to all of this, you must also be determined to heal from the trauma. When you develop a mindset of continuously growing, you shift your perspective towards what is good and healthy for you. It gives you less room to fall into that cycle of negative self-talk. You also celebrate your efforts and progress, which helps strengthen your sense of accomplishment.

Visualization techniques are also very helpful. You imagine yourself achieving these goals creates the mindset of setting realistic goals. It boosts confidence and prepares your mind for success. It also pushes the person to experience positive feelings, which in return creates motivation to feel said feelings again.

In order to not fall into setbacks, you have to build resilience. Resilience is the ability to bounce back from your fallouts. But bouncing back is not the only thing; you also need to have a positive outlook on these issues. When you have a positive outlook, you push yourself out of this comfort zone and create new hobbies that counter negative thought processes.

Working on bettering the environment is also important when you are going through a healing process. When the environment you live in helps establish routines and set boundaries, then you create a better chance for yourself not to fall back into those self-destructive tendencies.

Everything takes time to heal. This will not help you overnight. It was a process for you to develop these negative thoughts, so it will be a process for you to heal from them.

Chapter Seven

Boundaries

Boundaries are the limits or rules we set for ourselves in order to protect our well-being and ensure that we feel safe, respected, and valued. They serve as guidelines that help define what is acceptable and what is not in various aspects of our lives—whether in relationships, at work, within our families, or in personal spaces.

When I was 18, I had just become a mother to my first daughter. Life was a whirlwind. I was living with my mom and sister. The challenges of motherhood had me in a chokehold. At the time, I had recently reconnected with my dad, and my uncle was dying. It felt like everything in my world was in flux.

One day, my mom asked me to give my uncle my TV. It might sound small, but for me, at that moment, it felt like a huge request. My uncle had a broken TV, and because he was dying, my mom insisted it was the right thing to do. I was just 18, figuring out life, and already carrying the weight of being a new mom. I tried to refuse it, but my mom shot down my request and insisted I give it to my uncle because he was sick. I decided to comply, but my mom's words stung. She didn't just ask me for the TV—she made me feel guilty for even questioning it.

At that moment, I had no boundaries. I let her talk down to me and let her make decisions for me that I wasn't comfortable with. I didn't feel safe or respected in that moment. But I didn't know how to say no, so I gave the TV away, and it made me feel small and unseen.

Some boundaries are relatively straightforward to set. For example, telling a child not to touch a parent's car or asking a coworker not to leave their items on your desk. However, other boundaries can feel much more challenging, like telling a parent they can't drop in unannounced to visit a grandchild or asking a partner to respect your time for daily exercise. It can be especially difficult to insist that close friends or family members respect boundaries that they may not agree with, but doing so is often necessary to protect your balance and well-being.

Looking back, I realize that was a prime example of unhealthy boundaries. I allowed someone else's needs to take precedence over my own, even though my feelings and comfort mattered too. That moment set the stage for years of me struggling to establish healthy boundaries.

As I grew older and started to heal, I began to understand how crucial boundaries are in every part of life. Boundaries are not just about keeping others out; they are about protecting yourself, your mental space, your emotions, and your physical well-being. They are what help you feel safe, respected, and valued in all of your relationships.

Throughout my journey I have learned that boundaries have many forms to them. They can be physical, emotional, intellectual, and financial boundaries. Each aspect of your life has a boundary that caters to it. Having physical boundaries means that you set a limit on your personal space and physical interactions. You decide who can touch you, when, and where. For me, this was huge in my relationship with my family, especially with my mom. I had to learn how to say no when I didn't feel comfortable with how close someone was getting or how much space they were taking up in my life.

Some family members get away with touching you and labeling it as love when you only feel uncomfortable. This can be very frustrating. When you learn to say no, it's not just about stopping the action; it's also about knowing how to deal with the aftermath. Most people tend to have weak physical boundaries because it makes them more likable to the person invading them. 'Saying no might cause them not to like me' is the thought process for most of them. So, when you learn how to set physical boundaries, you learn how to deal with the consequences.

With relationships, lines can blur out in an instant because many emotions are involved. Setting emotional boundaries is also very important. They help you understand and protect your emotions. Emotional boundaries are like an invisible line that helps you keep your feelings your own. I had to learn that it wasn't my responsibility to manage the emotions of others, especially when those emotions were being used to manipulate or guilt me into things. I had to own and not let others make me feel bad about setting limits.

Often, people think that boundaries are just a way to make distance and keep people away, but they are more for you than for other people. Intellectual boundaries explain this in a better way. These boundaries involve respecting one another's ideas, opinions, and beliefs. Everyone is entitled to their own thoughts, and it's essential to respect that. I had to realize that my opinions, ideas, and values were just as important as anyone else's, and it was okay for me to stand firm in those beliefs, even if they didn't match up with someone else's.

Financial boundaries are, as the name suggests, related to your money and finances. People tend to be afraid to ask for money back once a loved one has borrowed some. Setting these boundaries in these types of relationships is crucial. People with weak financial boundaries are more prone to be taken advantage of. They easily get swept away and then face financial restraints in their own lives. You can also set financial boundaries for yourself. Unnecessary shopping sprees that lead to chaotic end-of-the-month budgeting are a sign of unhealthy financial boundaries.

Boundaries play an important role in shaping a person's way of interacting with people around them. Even within the different aspects of boundaries, people have different types of boundaries: Rigid, porous, and, in some cases, non-existent. These boundary types can affect a person's relationship, behavior in certain conditions, and overall well-being.

In terms of personal and physical boundaries, people who have rigid boundaries often avoid intimacy and close relationships. They prioritize control and independence, and in the process, they often put up walls that prevent others from getting close either emotionally or physically. This behavior may stem from past traumas, fear of vulnerability, or simply avoid conflict. People with rigid boundaries can often be highly self-reliant. They may come off as rude, mysterious, or even shy. For them, these interactions need to be carefully planned in order to keep people at arm's length. In some cases, people have difficulty forming meaningful connections. This leads to feelings of isolation and loneliness.

When it comes to emotional boundaries, a reluctance to share feelings or accept support and help can reflect signs of rigid boundaries. People with rigid emotional boundaries avoid opening up about their struggles, even with close friends and family members. They build these emotional walls that make them seem detached and isolated. In its essence, it can be a coping strategy for protection from potential hurt. Over time, the rigidity limits the ability to build trust in relationships and can lead to feelings of extreme loneliness and depression.

Having a rigid financial boundary can look like an extreme reluctance to spend money, even on things that can help improve life quality. A person with rigid financial boundaries might refuse to help a friend in dire need, even if he or she can afford to help. They also might avoid investing money into comfort or anything that adds to their well-being.

Boundaries also form in work life. In a professional setting, a person with rigid boundaries compartmentalize their personal and professional lives. They refuse to engage in workplace friendships or share any personal details with their colleagues. This can lead to social isolation and risk of potential work growth.

Rigid boundaries provide a sense of security and protection to the person, but unbeknownst to them, they affect personal growth, relationships, and overall life satisfaction. It is important to understand how to recognize behavior that can show patterns of a rigid boundary in any section of life. Dealing with a boundary is possible when you deal with the initial cause of that boundary. It takes time and energy to come out of your shell and let other people in.

Porous boundaries are less intense than rigid boundaries. While rigid boundaries emphasize control and distance, porous boundaries define excessive openness, lack of structure, and difficulty saying "no." People with porous boundaries often blur the line between themselves and others. They allow others to impact their decisions, emotions, and sometimes even their identities. With boundaries like these, people create challenges in their personal, emotional, physical, financial, and professional areas of life.

The more I understood these boundaries, the more I began to see how my past relationships were unhealthy because I didn't have any. Without boundaries, I found myself constantly people-pleasing, saying yes when I should have said no, and allowing others to take advantage of my time, space, and energy.

But once I started putting healthy boundaries in place, my life started to change. I became more aware of my own needs, and I stopped prioritizing everyone else's needs above my own. I stopped being afraid to say no, and I began to take ownership of my life and my decisions. My relationships started to shift, too.

I remember the first time I set a boundary with my teenage daughter. I had always been the "yes mom," giving her everything she asked for, from my car to my debit card. But at some point, I realized that I had to set clear, enforceable boundaries. I told her, "You can borrow my car, but I expect you to return it by 10 p.m. and fill it with gas." It wasn't about being strict; it was about showing respect for my belongings and for the rules we needed to follow as a family. It wasn't easy at first, but the more I enforced those boundaries, the more my daughter respected them.

Setting boundaries is a continual process, and it can be uncomfortable, especially when you're not used to it. I had to learn how to communicate them clearly and consistently. The more I practiced, the more I realized that boundaries don't close you off from others. In fact, they create space for healthier, more authentic relationships. They help you build trust, safety, and mutual respect.

The most challenging boundaries to establish tend to be within intimate relationships. A partner might cross boundaries by sharing private information without consent, disregarding work schedules, or even touching in ways that feel uncomfortable. But, with clear and well-communicated boundaries in place, couples can work on their selves and maintain a healthy relationship. Partners need to openly communicate their boundaries and avoid things that may cross the other person's set boundaries. By doing so, they can maintain their relationship in a much healthier way.

Boundaries are a fundamental part of our lives. They function as guidelines that define where one thing begins and the other ends. They help us establish limits on our own terms in all aspects of our lives, be it relationships, work, and daily interactions. Healthy boundaries allow us to protect our physical, emotional, and mental health. They also help us maintain healthy relationships with the people around us. These boundaries help us prioritize our needs and values with the absence of guilt or fear.

Rigid boundaries do provide a sense of security at first, but sooner or later, they lead to isolation. On the other hand, porous boundaries help you get into relationships and friendships faster. Still, often, these connections lack foundation and come at the expense of self-care and personal autonomy.

Making healthy boundaries requires self-awareness, good communication, and self-respect. Setting boundaries doesn't push people away; rather, it brings the right people closer. By maintaining healthy boundaries, we maintain better emotional and mental health.

For anyone struggling with setting boundaries, I would say this: You are allowed to say no. You are allowed to protect your emotional and physical space. You don't have to please everyone, and you don't have to be a martyr for others' happiness. Boundaries are a form of self-care, and you deserve to take care of yourself.

And one last thing: Respecting others' boundaries is just as important as setting your own. If you want others to respect your limits, you have to be willing to respect theirs. Healthy boundaries are a two-way street.

It's taken years to learn these lessons, but today, I can say that I've built a life that honors my needs. I'm no longer stuck in the cycle of people-pleasing, and I'm no longer afraid to protect my time, my energy, and my heart.

That's the power of healthy boundaries—they don't just protect you; they help you thrive.

Chapter Eight

Self-Knowledge, Self-Respect, Self-Love

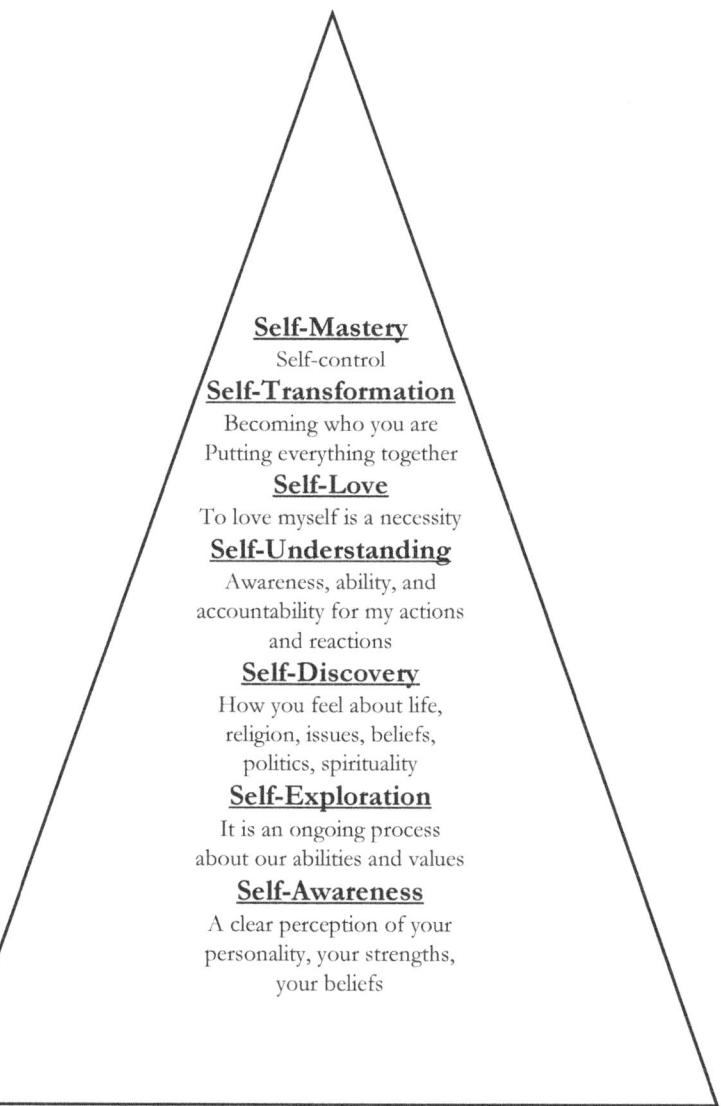

Self-Mastery
Self-control
Self-Transformation
Becoming who you are
Putting everything together
Self-Love
To love myself is a necessity
Self-Understanding
Awareness, ability, and
accountability for my actions
and reactions
Self-Discovery
How you feel about life,
religion, issues, beliefs,
politics, spirituality
Self-Exploration
It is an ongoing process
about our abilities and values
Self-Awareness
A clear perception of your
personality, your strengths,
your beliefs

Part I: Self-Knowledge

Self-knowledge is the deep understanding of your inner self. This includes your thoughts, emotions, motives, abilities, and character. It's more than figuring out surface-level information; rather, you dive into the core of who you are and what makes you a person. Self-knowledge always comes without any filter. You get to know both the positive and the uncomfortable aspects of yourself. You must have the willingness to confront and accept these aspects before going through the process. Self-knowledge is an ongoing process of reflection and growth. It evolves over time.

Understanding yourself is essential for personal growth and mental health. Self-knowledge helps you heal and make positive changes by identifying areas in your life that need improvement. It enhances decision-making by helping you identify your true needs, desires, and values, guiding you toward choices that align with your authentic self. Moreover, it fosters empathy and stronger relationships by enabling you to understand your emotions and relate to others on a deeper level. Without self-knowledge, it's easy to feel lost or make decisions that lead you further from fulfillment.

Self-awareness goes hand-in-hand with self-knowledge, but they are quite different in the way they dive into the depths of self-understanding. Self-awareness is the ability to observe and recognize your actions, emotions, and reactions in different situations. It's about focusing on how you behave, identifying common responses, and understanding the underlying reasons behind them. For instance, self-awareness can help you notice that you feel anxious in social settings or that you commonly procrastinate on important tasks.

Self-knowledge takes all of this and adds a deeper level of understanding. It's about uncovering the hidden reasons behind your actions, emotions, and beliefs. It asks why you feel or act a certain way, and in the process, it guides you to the core of who you are as a person. Self-knowledge enables you to examine your values, motivations, fears, and past experiences to gain insight into who you are as a person. If self-awareness is identifying your habit of procrastinating, then self-knowledge is understanding if it's rooted in perfectionism, fear of failure, or lack of interest.

However, both are important for personal growth. Self-awareness is mostly the first step. It helps you identify the behaviors and reactions in the present. It forms a baseline for building emotional intelligence and mindfulness. Self-knowledge involves a deeper commitment to introspection and vulnerability. It pushes you to confront your inner truths, regardless if they are uncomfortable. It also explores aspects of yourself that are not on the surface level or neglected.

Overall, self-awareness helps you with your superficial actions and responses, while self-knowledge shapes your deeper understanding of yourself. Together, they make a complete picture of you.

Sel-knowledge comes in two different types: active self-knowledge and passive-knowledge. Active self-knowledge is your ability to consciously assess situations and make intentional decisions within that moment. It's about implementing that understanding of yourself when you face challenges or opportunities. For example, active self-knowledge can involve identifying when you are getting overwhelmed and choosing to take a break to prevent possible burnout. It's a dynamic, real-time use of your self-understanding that helps you be in control. Active self-knowledge is really important in decision-making and problem-solving. It allows you to respond mindfully and not react impulsively.

Passive self-knowledge is the deeper understanding of your natural tendencies. You recognize your patterns and the way your actions influence others and your environment. It's all about being aware of how you normally respond to certain situations, triggers, or emotions. You also identify the impact of those responses. For example, you may realize that you might have the habit of withdrawing from conflict or confrontation or that your insight inspires others in your group. Passive self-knowledge doesn't involve immediate action or response. It helps you understand the bigger picture.

These two types of self-knowledge create a complete understanding of yourself. Active self-knowledge enables you to take charge of the present moment and then shape your future, while passive self-knowledge enables you to view your past behaviors and patterns. Both of these are necessary to achieve greater self-awareness, intentionality, and balance.

Building self-knowledge requires a lot of effort. Regular reflection is a key practice. It allows you to evaluate your thoughts, feelings, and actions. Another took to help this process is journaling. Journaling helps you uncover patterns as it gives you a sense of an outsider's perspective when you read back what you have written. One crucial step is facing your fears and addressing your past mistakes or insecurities. Growth comes from confronting the uncomfortable truths you may be unintentionally avoiding. Finally, evaluate key areas of your life, such as physical, emotional, mental, and spiritual well-being. This helps you to reveal what works and what needs work. The process of acquiring self-knowledge is a continuous one. It slowly starts to make its way into your routine thinking process. You look into everything with that mindset and uncover new details in your daily life.

The first step in building self-knowledge is self-awareness. At this stage, you start to have a clear perception of your personality. You are aware of what your strengths and weaknesses are and also what patterns of behavior bring them out. You observe how you interact with the world around you and how your behavior, emotions, and thoughts align. Self-awareness is the same as turning on a light in a room. You get to see what it is in its true form and identify areas that need attention.

To develop self-knowledge, we have to evaluate the physical, emotional, mental, and spiritual areas of our lives.

Part II: Self-Respect

There was a time when I didn't truly understand self-respect. I didn't know what it meant to respect myself. My actions betrayed my thoughts of respecting myself. Self-respect is the ability to value and affirm yourself even when you're facing self-doubt or are challenged. It's treating yourself with kindness and care and loving yourself.

It is a huge part of mental well-being. It has to do a lot with your pride, your confidence, and your feelings. Having self-respect helps you act with honor and dignity. You are aware of yourself and how you show yourself to the world. For years, I didn't see it that way. I struggled with feelings of inadequacy, constantly seeking validation from others and comparing myself to them. My boundaries were nonexistent—I'd say yes when I needed to say no, and I'd bend over backward to please people at the expense of my own happiness.

Negative self-talk became my constant companion. I'd put myself down and often disguised it as humor. Compliments felt foreign and undeserved. When someone told me I was pretty or mentioned my beautiful eyes, I'd brush it off. I didn't realize that this was a sign of lacking self-respect.

My goals were another reflection of my struggle. I'd set unrealistic ones, like planning to travel to Florida and Trinidad and fix my car all within six months. I knew it wasn't feasible on a single income but I still made these goals. Deep down, I knew they were unattainable, but somehow, failing to meet them felt safer than admitting they weren't realistic in the first place.

One day, a quote struck me:

No respect equals self-disrespect and self-negligence.

It hit me like a lightning bolt. If I couldn't respect myself, I was neglecting my own needs and undermining my worth. I knew I needed to change, not just for myself but for my relationships with others.

I started to examine the root causes of my lack of self-respect. Childhood trauma, fear of rejection, and a history of toxic shame from past mistakes were all contributors. I realized that my self-esteem had been eroded over time, leaving me feeling unworthy and unsupported.

But I wasn't ready to give up on myself. Slowly, I started to rebuild. Positive affirmations really helped. I wrote them on sticky notes and placed them on my bedroom mirror and inside my wallet. Each time I saw those words, they reminded me of my worth. Self-care was another essential step. I started doing Zumba and yoga regularly. Walking barefoot on the earth, meditating by the water, and simply being in nature helped me reconnect with myself.

Setting boundaries was the hardest lesson of all. I realized that respecting myself meant teaching others to respect me too. Even with my adopted children, I learned to enforce boundaries in the kitchen. It wasn't easy, especially when met with attitudes, but I stuck to it.

Even today, I'm still on this journey, but I've come a long way. My confidence has grown, and my voice is clearer. I speak my truth, express my needs, and honor my feelings. I've learned to accept compliments without deflecting, and I forgive myself for past mistakes.

Building self-respect is an ongoing process, and the rewards are immeasurable. It's not about perfection; it's about acceptance. It's about embracing who you are, flaws and all, and committing to growth.

I carry a simple but profound reminder in my wallet. With every step I take, I strive to honor that commitment, knowing that self-respect is the foundation for a life of dignity, authenticity, and love.

Commit to doing no harm, especially to yourself.

We have talked about how to take a step towards acquiring self-knowledge; well, the next step takes you to self-respect. It is self-exploration. This is where you begin to dig deeper into your inner self. You start to identify your values, beliefs, and emotional responses. It's a process of questioning. What do you stand for? What drives you? How do your emotions guide or misguide you? Through self-exploration, you gain clarity about what matters to you and how your experiences have shaped your perspective. This step requires curiosity and courage. You need a strong will as you may uncover aspects of yourself you haven't fully acknowledged.

55

The third step, Self-discovery, is pushing yourself to reflect on your beliefs about life, your purpose, and your place in the world. This stage is about looking beyond immediate concerns and considering the bigger picture of who you are and how you relate to the world around you. You might explore your spiritual beliefs, examine your goals, or contemplate the legacy you want to leave behind. Self-discovery usually brings insights that reshape the already existing aspects of your life.

Self-understanding is all about using the insights gained from earlier stages. Here, you develop a deeper awareness of how your thoughts, emotions, and behaviors interact and learn how to deal with challenging situations in a healthy way. This step equips you with tools to handle difficult situations, make calculated decisions, and manage relationships with greater ease. Self-understanding helps increase emotional intelligence which enables you to build much healthier relationships.

Part III: Self Love

Self-love was something I struggled with for much of my life. I thought I understood it, but in truth, I was just surviving, not thriving. Self-love is about having a positive regard for yourself, valuing your well-being, and appreciating yourself for who you are and all that you've been through. It's the way you show care for your physical, psychological, and spiritual growth. And yet, for years, I didn't give myself permission to experience it truly.

I learned that self-love isn't just about feeling good about yourself—it's about aligning your actions with your feelings, making choices that nurture you, and supporting your mental and spiritual journey. My responses and choices didn't always reflect that alignment, and that left me drained.

By the time I was 25, I thought I had it all. I had accomplished what many would call the American dream. I had purchased my first condo and my first SUV. I had my children settled in school in Darien, Connecticut. I worked for Greenwich Hospital, and everything in my life seemed to signal success. I thought, *this is it. There's nothing else I could possibly want.*

But the truth was, I found myself minimizing my achievements. I'd water down my accomplishments so others would feel more comfortable. I wouldn't share my successes, even with those closest to me. I did this out of fear of standing out or fear of making others feel inadequate.

But by dimming my light, I was only hurting myself. I took so much from myself by failing to celebrate my accomplishments and by failing to honor my journey. That's when I knew things needed to change. I needed to be authentic. I needed to embrace myself unapologetically.

I began the journey to rediscover myself, step by step. I started learning that being authentic meant having my own opinions, values, and beliefs without letting others sway or silence me. I had to learn how to be gentle and kind to myself, especially in moments of stress and impulsivity. For instance, writing this book has become a catalyst for change. It has forced me to slow down, to pause, and to respond.

Being calm, being present, and learning how to process emotions became vital. I began celebrating myself. I started celebrating the small blessings, the big blessings, and every moment of progress. Every day, I'd pause to thank my ancestors and count my blessings. "Thank you, God," became a mantra. I spent every day being grateful, and it brought me closer to my spiritual growth and closer to myself.

Setting boundaries was another lesson I had to learn the hard way. Boundaries, I've found, are at the heart of self-love. Without them, it becomes too easy to lose yourself in trying to please others or making sure everyone else is okay at your own expense. I learned that boundaries are not selfish. They are a way of respecting myself and creating a space where I can thrive.

I surrounded myself with positive, like-minded people. They genuinely cared for me and my journey. Being in the presence of love, encouragement, and shared growth became essential. And as I focused on self-love, I also focused on self-care. It became a ritual—

doing my hair, painting my nails, exploring new colors, treating myself to dinners, and taking long walks on the beach. Self-care became a non-negotiable, and it felt so good to put myself first in this way.

I also learned to recognize the signs that I lacked self-love. I saw how easy it was to slip into unhappiness, bitterness, hopelessness, and people-pleasing. I learned that ignoring my own needs in favor of everyone else's was only a way to avoid accountability—and without accountability, there could be no growth.

So, I started taking ownership of my actions, even the small ones. I meditated on them, sat with them, and came to terms with the fact that I had a role in every moment of my life. Sometimes, it wasn't easy to admit my mistakes or confront my fears, but I knew it was necessary.

Self-love was no longer just a distant concept. It became my daily practice, a journey of learning to trust myself, honor my path, and embrace my whole story—the good, the bad, the mistakes, and the successes.

Now, I know that self-love is a commitment. It's about being authentic, setting boundaries, cultivating gratitude, and taking care of my spiritual, emotional, and physical well-being. I've come to see that the journey doesn't end—it's continuous, and that's okay. Every step brings me closer to the person I've always deserved to be: at peace, authentic, and full of love.

And so, I continue this journey. I celebrate myself. I celebrate my blessings. I keep learning, growing, and loving. I didn't just grow in words, but in every action, every moment, every choice.

Because when you love yourself, you realize that you've always been enough.

Chapter Nine

Healing

Healing is the transformative process of restoring oneself to a state of wholeness and well-being. This covers all aspects of life: physical, mental, emotional, and spiritual. It is not merely the mending of physical wounds but also the rejuvenation of the mind, heart, and spirit. To heal is to overcome the undesirable conditions that life and trauma have imposed, allowing oneself to grow stronger and more resilient. This chapter delves into the multifaceted journey of healing, exploring its dimensions, principles, and practical steps for self-restoration.

It is about reclaiming your health, energy, and mental clarity, it is about becoming whole again. It is the journey of addressing past traumas and challenges, transforming pain into strength, and finding balance. Physical healing involves recovering from injuries like bruises, tissue damage, or joint issues, while mental, emotional, and psychological healing focuses on inner challenges such as thoughts, emotions, and perceptions. This form of healing often demands deep introspection and self-awareness. Spiritual healing, on the other hand, addresses spiritual weaknesses, negative energies, or feelings of disconnection. Practices like meditation, prayer, and mindfulness can be instrumental, particularly for those with religious or spiritual foundations.

The fundamental rule of healing is to "do no harm." This principle applies both to oneself and others. True healing cannot occur when harm is wished upon others or inflicted upon oneself. Instead, it requires a commitment to kindness, self-respect, and balance.

Healing is a deeply personal and ongoing process, and the journey often begins with self-love and care. Prioritize activities that nurture your body and soul, such as exercise, grooming, or spending time in nature. Practices like yoga, Zumba, or meditative walks near water can be profoundly therapeutic. Identifying the source of pain is equally important—whether it stems from a person, event, or recurring thought pattern, understanding its origin is essential for progress.

Building a support system can greatly aid the healing process. While close friends and family are invaluable, alternative resources such as podcasts, books, or online communities can also provide support. Gratitude for these resources fosters resilience and a positive mindset. Practicing mindfulness and gratitude further enhances healing, helping you stay present and focus on personal growth. Daily affirmations, accountability, and mindfulness can shift your perspective and promote a sense of peace.

Forgiveness is a cornerstone of healing. Begin by forgiving yourself for allowing hurtful situations to persist, then extend forgiveness to others, acknowledging their circumstances without condoning their actions. Letting go of the past is another crucial step. The past can only affect your present if you allow it to. By releasing its hold, you create space for growth and transformation.

Processing and releasing pain is essential to healing. Whether through crying, yelling, or physical outlets like boxing, it's important to allow yourself to feel and release pent-up emotions. This catharsis paves the way for growth and transformation. With newfound awareness, you can identify and avoid toxic environments, cultivate wisdom, and foster healthier relationships.

As healing progresses, it brings about profound transformation. You become a new person with an enhanced perspective on life and relationships. Boundaries are established, self-love is embraced, and you develop greater empathy for yourself and others. Healing fosters confidence, self-awareness, and an open-minded approach to challenges, allowing mistakes to become opportunities for growth rather than sources of shame.

Healing is essential for personal and collective evolution. It fosters balance across all aspects of life: physical, mental, emotional, social, spiritual, and even financial. Without healing, true growth and progress remain elusive. The timeline for healing varies widely. Some may find peace within months, while for others, it may take years.

Factors like environment and support systems play a significant role. Toxic spaces can stagnate progress, while proactive accountability and effort can accelerate it.

Ultimately, healing is an ongoing process—an evolution rather than a destination. Triggers may arise, but with self-awareness and the tools to manage them, they lose their power. Through healing, we gain clarity on what truly matters, enabling us to live authentically and fully. The journey of healing is a testament to human resilience and the boundless capacity for transformation.

In many different books, healing is described as a comprehensive and integrative process that addresses the impact of trauma on the mind, brain, and body. According to Dr. Bessel van der Kolk, trauma leaves lasting imprints not only on memory but also on the body's physiological and neurological systems. As such, true healing requires a holistic approach that reconnects individuals with themselves on multiple levels, helping them regain a sense of safety, control, and self-awareness.

In the process of healing, the mind-body connection is very important. Trauma often disrupts this harmony, causing people to feel disconnected from their physical selves. Practices such as yoga, mindfulness, and even theater are presented as powerful tools to restore this connection, allowing the body to release the tension and fear it holds onto. These somatic therapies complement traditional psychological methods, highlighting the need for a multidimensional approach to trauma recovery.

The concept of neuroplasticity is also emphasized, which is the brain's ability to rewire itself. Trauma alters the way the brain processes information, often leading to hypervigilance, emotional dysregulation, and repetitive cycles of distress. Healing harnesses the brain's natural adaptability, utilizing therapies like EMDR (Eye Movement Desensitization and Reprocessing), neurofeedback, and other innovative treatments to help survivors regain control over their thoughts and emotions.

A crucial aspect of healing, as outlined in the book, is the process of owning and expressing one's story. Trauma often silences individuals and traps them in feelings of shame or helplessness. Healing begins when people can safely confront and articulate their pain, transforming past suffering into an opportunity for growth and self-discovery. Through supportive environments and tailored interventions, survivors can reclaim their lives and move forward with resilience.

Ultimately, researches underscore the necessity of a compassionate and personalized approach to healing. It is not just about addressing symptoms but about helping individuals restore their inner sense of balance and well-being, paving the way for a more connected and fulfilling life.

Healing from trauma often involves a variety of therapeutic approaches that address the physical, emotional, and psychological dimensions of well-being. Each therapy serves a unique purpose, and their effectiveness often depends on the individual's specific needs and trauma history. In *The Body Keeps the Score*, Dr. Bessel van der Kolk emphasizes the importance of using integrative therapies that cater to both the mind and the body.

Psychotherapy is one of the most common methods for trauma recovery. Cognitive Behavioral Therapy (CBT) focuses on identifying and reframing negative thought patterns, helping individuals understand the relationship between their thoughts, emotions, and behaviors. Eye Movement Desensitization and Reprocessing (EMDR) is another widely used approach. By guiding individuals through controlled eye movements while revisiting traumatic memories, EMDR helps to reduce their emotional intensity and reprocess the trauma. Internal Family Systems (IFS) therapy explores and heals the different parts of oneself, such as the "inner child" or "protector" roles, fostering self-compassion and internal harmony.

Somatic therapies are equally important, as trauma often manifests physically. Yoga and movement therapy reconnect the mind and body, allowing individuals to release stored tension and improve body awareness. Somatic Experiencing (SE), developed by Dr. Peter Levine, focuses on processing physical sensations rather than delving deeply into narratives. This gradual, body-centered approach helps release the pent-up energy associated with trauma, restoring a sense of safety and calm.

Neurofeedback and other brain-based therapies help regulate the brain's responses to trauma. Neurofeedback trains the brain to manage its activity, calming hyperactive "fight or flight" responses that are common in trauma survivors. Mindfulness-Based Stress Reduction (MBSR) is another effective tool, teaching individuals to stay present and detach from intrusive thoughts. By cultivating awareness of the here and now, mindfulness promotes emotional regulation and reduces stress.

Expressive therapies like art, drama, and music therapy provide creative outlets for processing emotions. Art therapy allows individuals to express feelings they may struggle to articulate verbally. Drama therapy, through role-play and storytelling, helps participants reframe their trauma and explore new perspectives. Music therapy, whether through listening or creating, can soothe the mind, regulate emotions, and stimulate emotional processing.

Body-centered therapies like massage and acupuncture address the physical toll of trauma. Massage helps individuals reconnect with their bodies, fostering relaxation and releasing tension. Acupuncture, by balancing the body's energy, can reduce symptoms of anxiety and depression, promoting overall well-being.

Relational therapies, such as group therapy and attachment-based therapy, help rebuild trust and connection. Group therapy provides a safe space to share experiences with others who have faced similar challenges, reducing feelings of isolation and shame. Attachment-based therapy focuses on healing relational trauma by strengthening secure connections with others.

Finally, narrative therapy empowers individuals to reconstruct their life stories in ways that integrate their trauma and highlight resilience. By reclaiming control over their personal narratives, survivors can shift their perspective from one of victimhood to one of growth and strength.

These diverse therapies offer a range of tools for healing. Often, a combination of approaches tailored to the individual's circumstances yields the most effective results, supporting the journey toward recovery and resilience.

Healing is not a one-time achievement or a destination to be reached; it is an ongoing, evolving process that unfolds throughout life. Traumas and challenges leave imprints on our minds, bodies, and spirits, and while significant strides can be made through therapy, self-reflection, and supportive practices, the journey of healing is dynamic. It requires continual attention, adaptation, and effort as new experiences and insights shape our growth.

One of the primary reasons healing is continuous is that life is ever-changing, and we encounter new circumstances that may test old wounds or open new ones. Events such as relationship changes, career challenges, or even small triggers can resurface unresolved emotions or memories. These moments are not setbacks but opportunities to deepen the healing process, reinforcing the tools and resilience we have developed.

Moreover, healing is about growth rather than simply erasing pain. As we heal, we gain new perspectives, self-awareness, and coping mechanisms that allow us to navigate life's complexities with greater ease. This growth often reveals additional layers of healing. For example, forgiving oneself or others might feel like the final step in recovery, but as we evolve, we may discover deeper levels of forgiveness or understanding that further transform our emotional landscape.

The continuous nature of healing also reflects the human capacity for transformation. Just as trauma can alter us profoundly, so too can healing open doors to resilience, creativity, and compassion. Each stage of the healing process builds upon the last, creating a foundation for greater well-being and a more profound connection to ourselves and others.

It is also important to recognize that healing is not linear. Some days may feel like breakthroughs, while others may bring challenges or reminders of past struggles. This ebb and flow are natural and part of the process. Healing involves learning to accept these fluctuations, trusting that even in moments of difficulty, progress is being made.

Ultimately, viewing healing as a continuous journey rather than a finite task reframes it as an integral part of life. It becomes less about "fixing" ourselves and more about embracing the lifelong practice of self-care, growth, and self-discovery. This perspective not only alleviates the pressure to "get over" pain but also empowers us to live authentically, continually striving for balance and wholeness.

In *The Body Keeps the Score*, Dr. Bessel van der Kolk presents numerous examples of how healing transforms the lives of trauma survivors, demonstrating that recovery is not only possible but life-changing. These stories illustrate how individuals can regain control, reconnect with themselves and others, and build a life beyond trauma.

One compelling example involves veterans suffering from post-traumatic stress disorder (PTSD). Many had become emotionally numb, struggling to connect with their families or experience joy due to the overwhelming burden of their traumatic memories. Through therapies like Eye Movement Desensitization and Reprocessing (EMDR) and group therapy, they were able to process their trauma safely and effectively. These interventions helped the veterans re-establish emotional bonds with their loved ones, allowing them to reduce feelings of isolation and reconnect with the present instead of reliving the pain of their past.

Another poignant story in the book describes a woman who endured childhood sexual abuse and suffered from severe flashbacks and a persistent sense of danger. Her journey to healing involved somatic therapies like yoga, which allowed her to reconnect with her body and distinguish between the threats of the past and the safety of the present. Over time, she gained a greater sense of control over her physical and emotional responses, significantly reducing her symptoms and enabling her to face life with newfound confidence and ease.

The book also shares examples of individuals who turned to substance abuse or self-harm to cope with their trauma. For these individuals, therapies like neurofeedback and mindfulness practices provided effective ways to regulate their nervous systems and reduce the overwhelming stress that fueled their destructive behaviors. One patient reflected on how these tools helped replace harmful coping mechanisms with healthier ones, leading to a more stable and fulfilling life.

Storytelling is another powerful tool for healing discussed in the book. One patient, who had long suppressed memories of childhood abuse, found healing through narrative therapy and group discussions. Being able to articulate their experiences for the first time allowed them to confront their pain and release feelings of shame. By owning their story, they reclaimed their sense of identity and transformed their suffering into a source of strength and resilience.

Children are not excluded from the healing journey. Dr. van der Kolk describes a traumatized child exhibiting extreme behavioral issues and emotional disconnection. Participating in theater and role-play provided a safe space to explore suppressed feelings and emotions creatively. These activities helped the child restore emotional balance, express themselves healthily, and re-establish connections with others, demonstrating how healing can foster emotional growth and relational well-being.

Finally, the book emphasizes the profound impact of integrative approaches to healing. Many patients who engaged in a combination of therapies—such as EMDR, yoga, neurofeedback, and traditional talk therapy—reported significant improvements in their mental and emotional health. These interventions addressed the trauma\u2019s impact on the brain, body, and emotions, leading to a holistic transformation. Patients shared how they felt more grounded, emotionally resilient, and capable of embracing life fully, shifting from mere survival to thriving.

These examples highlight the transformative power of healing. Whether through reconnecting with loved ones, gaining emotional regulation, or reclaiming a sense of identity, the healing process enables trauma survivors to overcome their pain and build a life of growth, fulfillment, and resilience. The stories underscore the importance of a comprehensive and individualized approach to healing, showcasing the human spirit\u2019s extraordinary capacity for recovery.

www.ingramcontent.com/pod-product-compliance
Lightning Source LLC
Chambersburg PA
CBHW051238120626

46547CB00014B/1696